Routledge Revivals

Negotiation

First published in 1993, *Negotiation* places recent theoretical work on legal negotiation in a practical context. Negotiation skills are essential to every lawyer. Dealing chapter by chapter with planning for negotiation, verbal and non-verbal skills for the negotiator and the stages of a typical negotiation, the reader is invited to practice negotiation through an analysis of a real-life negotiation transcript and a variety of case studies of increasing complexity. This is an important book for students of legal studies.

Negotiation

Diana Tribe

Routledge
Taylor & Francis Group

First published in 1993
by Cavendish Publishing Limited

This edition first published in 2025 by Routledge
4 Park Square, Milton Park, Abingdon, Oxon, OX14 4RN

and by Routledge
605 Third Avenue, New York, NY 10017

Routledge is an imprint of the Taylor & Francis Group, an informa business

A Library of Congress record exists under ISBN: 1874241414

ISBN: 978-1-041-06187-8 (hbk)
ISBN: 978-1-003-63421-8 (ebk)
ISBN: 978-1-041-06188-5 (pbk)

Book DOI 10.4324/9781003634218

Negotiation

Diana Tribe

Series Editor
JULIE MACFARLANE

Cavendish
Publishing
Limited

First published in Great Britain 1993 by Cavendish Publishing Limited,
23A Countess Road, London NW5 2XH.
Telephone: 071-485 0303 Facsimile: 071-485 0304

British Library Cataloguing in Publication Data

Tribe, D
Negotiation - (Essential Legal Skills Series)
I Title II Series
344.2055

ISBN 1-874241-41-4

Contents

Practical Exercises for the Reader

Editor's Introduction

'The essence of our lawyer's craft lies in skills ...; in practical, effective, persuasive, inventive skills for getting things done ...'

Karl Llewellyn

The appearance of this new series of texts on legal skills reflects the recent shift in emphasis in legal education away from a focus on teaching legal information and towards the teaching and learning of task-related and problem-solving skills.

Legal education in the United Kingdom has undergone significant changes over the past ten years as a result of growing concern, expressed for the most part by the profession, over its adequacy to prepare students for the practice of law. At the same time, many legal educators have voiced fears that concentrating on drilling students in substantive law promotes neither the agility of mind nor the development of judgment skills which provide the basis for continued learning.

Today courses providing clinical experience and instruction in legal skills are increasingly a part of undergraduate law programmes. Both branches of the profession in England and Wales have fundamentally revised the content and format of their qualifying courses to include direct instruction in practical skills. In Scotland, the Diploma in Legal Practice, which emphasises the learning of practical skills, has been in place since 1980/81.

Nonetheless, legal skills education in the United Kingdom is still in its infancy. Much is to be learned from other jurisdictions which have a longer history of the use of practical and experience-based teaching methods, lessons invaluable to UK law teachers many of whom now face the challenge of developing new courses on legal skills. The ready exchange of ideas between skills teachers in the United Kingdom and abroad is an important part of the development process. So too is the generation of 'home-grown' texts and materials designed specifically for legal skills education in undergraduate and professional schools in the United Kingdom.

The introduction of skills teaching into the legal education curriculum has implications not only for what students learn in law school but also for how they learn. Similarly it has implications for the kind of textbooks which will be genuinely useful to students who wish to succeed in these programmes.

This new series of texts seeks to meet this need. Each text leads the reader through a stage-by-stage model of the development of a particular legal skill; from planning, through implementation in a variety of guises, to evaluation of performance. Each contains numerous practical exercises and guides to improve practice. Each draws on a network of theories about effective legal practice and relates theory to practice where that is useful and relevant.

The authors are all skills teachers with many years of practical experience at all levels of legal education. They draw on relevant literature and practice from all over the common law world. However each book is written specifically for students of law and legal practice in the United Kingdom and sets learning in the context of English law and against the backdrop of the Law Society's standards for the new Legal Practice Courses, due to commence in 1993/4.

Each of these texts is designed for use either as a supplement to a legal skills course taught at an undergraduate or professional level, or as a model for the structure and content of the course itself. We recommend the use of these books, therefore, to students and skills teachers alike, and hope that you enjoy them.

Julie Macfarlane
London, Ontario
February 1993

Introduction

This text is concerned with the legal skill of negotiation, which is essential to lawyers. In this country the vast majority of claims are settled prior to trial. The Green Paper on the Work and Organisation of the Legal Profession published in 1989 proposed that those training as lawyers should learn negotiating skills.

Whilst the importance of training intending lawyers in negotiation skills was recognised in the United States from the early 1950s, in the United Kingdom instruction in negotiation methods and techniques was not introduced into (some) undergraduate law programmes until about ten years ago. Only very recently has negotiation become a required element of the professional stage of training.

This text has been designed in three main sections. It moves the reader forward from an examination of theoretical models of negotiation and the basic negotiation process, to an 'observation' and evaluation of a negotiation, and finally to practice and self-evaluation. The first chapter examines the three main styles of negotiation, ie competitive, co-operative and problem-solving, and provides a brief theoretical underpinning to the following chapters. This is followed in Chapters 2, 3 and 4 by a consideration of the importance of verbal and non-verbal skills in the negotiation process, an outline of the preparatory planning stages which must be undertaken prior to a successful negotiation, and a linear account of a typical negotiation.

By this stage the reader should have formed a good theoretical understanding of the negotiation process. Chapter 5 introduces a transcript of a negotiation in a personal injury claim, where the reader acts as it were as 'observer', linking the earlier sections to this account of practice, and evaluating the performance of the negotiators.

In part three, Chapter 6 gives the reader the opportunity to practice negotiation through case studies while Chapter 7 describes more sophisticated techniques that can be used by the experienced negotiator. Finally Chapter 8 helps the reader to evaluate her performance as a negotiator. Commentary on the case studies is provided in Chapter 9.

Each chapter includes suggestions for further reading and provides questions (with answers) to check reader understanding, or exercises with suggested solutions.

Diana Tribe
February 1993

CHAPTER 1

What is Negotiation?

'Negotiation: to confer with another for the purpose of arranging some matters by mutual agreement; to discuss a matter with a view to settlement or compromise.'

Shorter Oxford Dictionary, 1977

1.1 Disputes

In life there is no shortage of disputes, for they occur at all levels: between husband and wife, between neighbours, between employees and their employers, between developers and environmentalists, between groups within a nation state and between nations themselves. Equally there are many ways of settling such disputes; some are private occurring behind closed doors, or are settled by the law of market supply and demand, while others are settled by established rituals occurring in legal or quasi-legal contexts. Whatever the process of settlement, be it formal or informal, successful or unsuccessful, there arises at some stage the need for the skill of bargaining or what will be described in this text as 'negotiation'.

The word 'negotiate' is here defined as the interactive social process in which people engage, when they aim to reach an agreement with another party (or parties), on behalf of themselves or another.

Thus an agreement between passengers on a train that a window should be kept open during the journey, or between work colleagues as to the use of car parking space, will typically be arrived at as a result of an inter-personal transaction which is commonly described as 'negotiation'. These two examples illustrate the simplest form of negotiation between individuals, where each explains his or her personal needs in relation to a particular social situation to the other, and resolves any needs or conflicts through compromise and bargaining activities. More complex negotiating processes occur, for example, between Trades Unions and management with the aim of reaching agreement on conditions of service for employees. Negotiation also takes place in political contexts; for example between politicians and interest groups, or between terrorists and police negotiating for the safe return of hostages.

Negotiation is a daily occurrence for all of us, occurring in employment, social and domestic contexts. It is also an important lawyering task, and is so much a integral part of a lawyer's daily professional life that in the past it was rarely recognised as a necessary skill or process. Today, this view is changing: it is now well known that less than 10% of disputes actually go to trial, the majority of cases being settled by negotiation at early or later stages of the pre-trial process. To say that most cases are settled does not however, imply that the potential for litigation is unimportant, for it is the possibility of litigation that provides the leverage that pushes opposing parties into settlement negotiations. It also provides, through the prediction of trial outcomes, the base line for assessing a value for individual cases. If you can achieve a settlement through negotiation you can save costs and time, and achieve good results for your client (see the Green Paper on 'The Work and Organisation of the Legal Profession' January 1989).

1.2 Can negotiating skills be learned?

Clearly some lawyers are much more skilled as negotiators than others, and while some individuals may have a natural talent as negotiators, it has been acknowledged for some time that training can develop and improve an individual's negotiating skills. To this end, many training manuals on negotiation have already been written, some of which borrow heavily from the study of bargaining by social psychologists (see for example Fisher and Ury 'Getting to Yes' (1981)). Such texts seem to suggest that the selection of a particular model of negotiation will lead to negotiation strategies which can be consistently successful, regardless of the social or occupational context in which that negotiation occurs.

This text is designed specifically for lawyers who negotiate. Over the past ten years negotiation as a lawyering process has emerged as a separate and legitimate subject for study and teaching at both the academic and professional stage of training in the United Kingdom. This recognition of the importance of negotiation skills for intending lawyers rests on the premise that a body of knowledge exists which can assist lawyers in becoming more effective negotiators.

1.3 The main styles of negotiation

An analysis of the literature indicates that at least three main styles of negotiation are commonly utilised, each style in its turn giving rise to the use of appropriate strategies. These strategies are not necessarily unique to specific styles, being capable of being used interchangeably. The three main styles however are clearly distinguishable, each having distinct objectives; for convenience they are described here as the 'competitive', the 'co-operative' and the 'problem-solving' styles, although since there is no universally accepted typology of these styles, the student may find them described differently elsewhere.

1.3.1 The competitive style of negotiation

Most of the early texts used in law schools as a basis for teaching negotiation, were based on the competitive (sometimes called the adversarial or zero-sum) style. The courtroom litigation model dominates in this version of negotiation, where zero-sum is defined as a situation where the total winnings for one party minus the total losses for the other party equal zero: thus what one party gains another must lose in a situation where resources are essentially limited and must be divided between parties.

'It is assumed that the parties must be in conflict and since they are presumed to be bargaining for the same scarce items, negotiators assume that any solution is predicated upon division of the goods.'

(Menkel-Meadow 1984)

Thus the competitive negotiator makes concessions reluctantly because they may 'weaken his position' through position loss or image loss. He tends to make high initial demands, few concessions and have a generally high level of aspiration for his client.

This competitive model makes the evaluation of a negotiation result easy; with only a 50:50 chance of achieving either of the bipolar results (win all: lose all), the compromise point achieves a result, without the transaction costs of trial. This result is likely to be the mid-point between the demands of each party, achieved after an appropriate period of negotiation. The competitive style is, therefore, most often used with success in simple negotiations over one issue such as the price in a buy/sell negotiation, or money damages in a personal injury or breach of contract action.

It is often suggested that this style leads practitioners into specific negotiation strategies, for example, never making the first offer, always attempting to conceal the client's true objectives, always being the person who drafts the final offer; and the use of exaggeration, threat and bluff to create high levels of tension and pressure on the opponent. If used effectively these tactics cause the opposing side to lose confidence in their case and reduce their expectations of what can be obtained for their client. It is therefore, an essentially manipulative approach, designed to intimidate the opposing side into accepting a negotiator's demands.

These competitive strategies have a number of limitations however. They may force parties into defensive positions, thus inhibiting the development of new or creative solutions. The competitive style can also lead to serious disadvantages for the competitive negotiator and her client, if the other side responds in kind to this strategy, fails to implement the decision finally agreed upon, or feels resentful towards the opposing negotiator in future negotiations. Other dangers of this approach include the possibility that in repeated encounters it will be increasingly unsuccessful, yielding a greater number of cases which will eventually go to trial.

1.3.2 The co-operative style of negotiation

Where the competitive negotiator seeks to force the opposing party to a favourable settlement, by convincing her opponent that his case is not as strong as he had previously thought, the co-operative style encourages a negotiator to make concessions, to build trust in the other party, and encourage him in turn to make further concessions. Each negotiator makes concessions in the anticipation that his opponent will reciprocate, and that the parties will then move to a compromise solution.

Co-operative negotiators move psychologically towards their opponents trying to establish a common ground, and seeking the highest joint outcome in which both parties may benefit. Concessions are made in anticipation that the opposing negotiator will reciprocate and that the parties will move closer to a compromise solution.

In this type of negotiation style, strategies which are typically used include the making of concessions, the sharing of information and the adoption of behaviours which are fair and reasonable. Thus a co-operative negotiator typically explains the reasons for her concessions and proposals and attempts to reconcile the parties' conflicting interests; her proposals are measured against standards which both parties can agree, such as the legal merits of the case and fairness between the parties.

The advantages of the co-operative style of negotiation are that it tends to produce fewer breakdowns in bargaining with subsequent recourse to litigation, and to produce more favourable outcomes for both parties. This leaves both clients and negotiators in a position where they can 'do business' again.

However, the co-operative style is subject to certain difficulties in operation where the parties to the negotiation are unequal in wealth or power or where one party will not bargain for joint or mutual gain; thus co-operative negotiation with agents of the government or of large corporations or extremely wealthy individuals (who have no incentive to look for mutual gain) may be difficult to achieve. Moreover, where a co-operative negotiator attempts to use this style in a negotiation with a tough non co-operative opponent the competitive negotiator tends to accept all the concessions made without offering anything in return.

1.3.3 The problem-solving (or integrative) style of negotiation

In 1981 Fisher and Ury published their seminal text 'Getting to Yes: Agreement Without Giving In' in which they advanced an alternative co-operative style called 'principled negotiation' which is claimed to be a universal, problem-solving approach that can be used in any negotiation context. It is not a concession-based approach seeking to allocate a fixed quantity of resources; instead it seeks to maximise the parties' potential for problem-solving, in order to increase the joint benefit and expand the quantity of resources. Like the co-operative style referred to in 1.3.2 above, this approach also aims to create a non-adversarial atmosphere in which the parties can work towards an agreement. Apart from this tactic, however, the styles are very different. The problem-solving style aims to maximise the parties' potential for problem-solving to increase the potential joint benefit for their clients. This style is usually associated with a situation in which the parties' interests are not directly opposed and where the parties invent a solution which satisfies both their interests.

> '... (it) is an orientation to negotiation which focuses on finding solutions to the parties' set of underlying needs and objectives.'
>
> (Menkel-Meadow 1984)

The process of discovering the parties' underlying needs and objectives can lead to the creation of more potential solutions, since the parties' needs need not be mutually exclusive. For example, in a personal injury action it is not always the case that the only issue at stake is the level of monetary compensation; it is well known that litigants sometimes need their 'day in court' for psychological reasons which are linked to their ability to recover more fully from the trauma of accident and litigation. In the commercial context an action for breach of contract may involve not simply monetary compensation for the cost of obtaining substitute goods but also issues relating to loss of future business and business reputation. By examining the weight or value given by the parties to their different needs and objectives, one side can increase its options in a negotiation without necessarily reducing those for the other side. This is in stark contrast to the zero-sum model where gain for one party must necessarily be a loss for the other.

Consider the following examples.

A problem-solving approach to a dispute over access might be based on the assumption that whilst both parents want access to their children for some of the time, neither would, in practice, want access for the whole of the time. On this basis a negotiated settlement advantageous to all parties (including the children) may be effected.

Another example of a problem-solving approach from a commercial context would be where one party wishes to make deferred payment over time, because of a lack of funds, whilst the other party may be willing to accept staged payments, for tax reasons.

The problem-solving approach thus commences with both negotiators trying to ascertain the underlying needs of their clients. This can best be achieved through client interviews in which the lawyer explores with the client how he wants the dispute to be concluded in social, economic, ethical and psychological terms. Focusing on the actual (rather than the assumed) needs of clients leads to solutions often more complex and yet more satisfactory in terms of social justice than those which a court could order, or which could result from competitive negotiation.

The four basic tactics which Fisher and Ury describe as being essential to the process of problem-solving negotiation are :

- separate the people from the problem; in other words, separate the interpersonal relationship between the negotiators and/or their clients from the merits of the problem or conflict
- focus on interests not positions; that is, consider the interests of the clients so that each party's motives, goals and values are fully understood by each side
- generate a variety of options; for example, brainstorm to develop new ideas to meet the needs of the parties
- insist that the result of the negotiation be based on some objective standard that is, assess proposed outcomes against easily ascertainable standard based on objective criteria

1.4 Which style to adopt?

The student who wishes to study negotiation styles is faced at the outset with (at least) the three possible models described above; each is claimed by some experts to be superior to the other two and this confusion is made worse by the fact that there is little consistency in the use of terminology in the literature (for example, non-competitive strategies are variously referred to as collaborative, co-operative and problem-solving).

An additional practical difficulty is that it may be appropriate during the course of a negotiation for a negotiator to use a combination of the these three broad approaches, since they are not necessarily mutually exclusive. Frequently a negotiator will use more than one style during a negotiation. Indeed it can be argued that a negotiator must chose between engaging in competitive behaviour, making a concession or suggesting an integrative proposal at each separate stage of a negotiation process. It seems inappropriate, therefore, for a legal negotiator to style herself as competitive, co-operative or problem-solving in approach, since all three of these styles may be variously utilised by a skilled negotiator at different stages in the settlement of a particular dispute.

In the end the selection of styles and associated strategies is relevant only in so far as they are employed as a means to achieve the objectives of the negotiation; it is the extent to which these objectives are actually achieved which will provide a measure of a negotiator's effectiveness.

1.5 What is an effective negotiator?

Is the most effective negotiator the lawyer who achieves the highest possible financial settlement on behalf of an injured client, or is it the lawyer who comes closest to achieving the average (and thus socially more equitable) award in a particular case? Alternatively, should effectiveness be determined by reference to client demands and expectations, or by reference to non-client related issues such as those of justice or public interest?

Clearly anyone who attempts to assess the effectiveness of a individual negotiator must consider the objectives of the legal system as a whole, as well as those of lawyers working within the system. While individual lawyers may be justified in energetically pursuing their clients' claims, even to the detriment of the opposing side, it is arguable that a wider perspective should consider the legitimate interests of all parties and of society as a whole. Assessing effectiveness and 'success' in negotiation is, as you can see, a highly complex business.

Factors which you may like to consider in determining the effectiveness of a negotiation could include:

- the financial outcome for the client
- the costs in time, money and general psychological wear and tear, on the client and /or the defendant in achieving the settlement
- the number of issues left unresolved at the end of the negotiation

- the potential stability of the agreement
- the relationship between the parties at the end of the negotiation
- the relationship between the negotiators at the end of the negotiation
- the eventual recognition between the parties that litigation or some other method of dispute resolution is necessary after all

1.6 Advantages and disadvantages of negotiation as settlement strategy

In general, settlement through negotiation offers a number of potential benefits to the parties involved. It may avoid the delays, economic costs and uncertainty associated with trial, and the 'winner takes all' nature of most legal remedies. Furthermore, negotiation reduces the pressure on trial courts, thus benefiting those plaintiffs whose cases do require litigation.

However, where a client is seeking new developments or clarification of the law, or feels personally affronted and needs the psychological benefit of his 'day in court', or where the action against a client is frivolous and brought only for its nuisance value, then there is a presumption against negotiation. Similarly, where the issue of liability or damages is so uncertain that you would prefer to shift the burden of evaluation to the courts, or where the opposing side is unwilling to compromise or accept negotiated solutions, a case should proceed to trial.

1.7 The effect of the negotiator's personality

Some negotiators find it easier to adopt one style rather than another, and this is said to be related to the psychological characteristics of the individual negotiator. Research indicates (Berkowitz 1968) that negotiators who exhibit personality traits such as authoritarianism, high self esteem, risk aversion and strong internal control are more likely to choose a competitive approach. On the other hand, those who are more reflective, and who can recognise the innate complexities of situations tend to adopt a non-competitive approach. Thus, a solicitor who is able to develop trust, and who forms good working relationships with others, is likely to be most effective as a co-operative negotiator.

It can perhaps be concluded that a negotiator cannot comfortably adopt a style which is fundamentally opposed to her normal interpersonal style, although no doubt it is possible to do so for short periods.

1.8 Case study

Mr and Mrs Bennett decide to have a conservatory built on to their house and employ a small firm, H&G Builders to carry out the work. It is agreed that the cost of the conservatory, which will be completed no later than the end of May, will be £17,500 including VAT, to be paid in three stages.

H&G Builders plan to commence the building of the conservatory in early March, but, due to the illness of one of the partners and the over running of another contract (a school extension for the local education authority) they do not in fact commence work until April, and the conservatory is not eventually completed until late June.

It is now August and Mr and Mrs Bennett have failed to make the third stage payment of £7,000 (due on completion), on the grounds that the work was not completed in time, the fitting of electrical plugs and light switches has not been carried out and bare wires have been left protruding from the wall.

Mr Goodison, a partner in H&G Builders, claims that the Bennetts were told at the outset that they would need to employ an electrician after the builders had left the site, to fit plugs and switches, and that it was their practice not to include such work in any agreement. However, there is no evidence of this in the (scanty) documentation currently available. Mr Goodison is anxious to recover the final £7,000 as soon as possible, as the firm operates on a very slim profit margin and he has to meet bills from timber suppliers before he can embark on new contracts.

He cannot afford for the case to go to trial and in any case the publicity which such a trial might generate would not be in the best interests of his firm.

Questions

a) assume you are negotiating with the Bennetts' solicitor on behalf of Mr Goodison. What style of negotiation would be likely to prove most effective in this situation? On what basis do you make this decision? Compare your reaction with that of your colleagues.

b) if the solicitor for Mr and Mrs Bennett pursues a non-competitive style does that leave you with a completely free choice as to which style you can adopt?

c) who should make the final choice of negotiation style?

1.9 Comments on case study

a) how to decide which style to chose?

The single most important factor in deciding between a competitive and a non-competitive style is the likely style of your opponent. To be successful, the co-operative and the problem-solving approaches require that negotiator and opponent both adopt the same approach. Thus a negotiator who is paired against a competitive opponent should not attempt a co-operative style; she will be exploited if she does so, as a competitive opponent will interpret her concessions as a sign of weakness and thus grant fewer concessions himself. A co-operative style thus succeeds only if the opponent reciprocates and makes concessions also.

The problem-solving style is rather less vulnerable to exploitation by a competitive negotiator since instead of proceeding by offering concessions it proceeds by offering new deals for creative solutions. Nevertheless problem-solving also requires an exchange of information and a responsiveness to the other negotiator's needs. This too may be exploited by a competitive negotiator, who may refuse to participate in the process of problem-solving.

The less powerful you are as a negotiator the more likely it is that you should chose a non-competitive style; the competitive style will fail for the low power negotiator since his threats are not credible.

In this problem the solicitor acting for Mr Goodison is not in a powerful position; the Bennetts can wait indefinitely to pay their bill as the conservatory is more or less completed. No doubt they have had the electrical work carried out for a reasonable sum, and are currently enjoying their extension during the summer weather. Mr Goodison on the other hand needs his money badly if he is to meet his obligations to other clients, and keep his firm in profit. He will not wish to be involved in (possibly) lengthy and (certainly) expensive litigation, to recover an unpredictable sum of money.

A possible solution might be to offer to deduct from the sum owed, the cost of any electrical work carried out for the Bennetts and a negotiated figure to represent the late completion. This can only be achieved however, if the other side is willing to adopt a co-operative or problem-solving style. However, the opposing solicitor may be aware of the likelihood that you and he may have future dealings with each other, and may try to persuade the Bennetts to adopt a more accommodating stance with that possibility in mind.

b) if your opponent pursues a non-competitive style does that leave you with a free choice as to which style to adopt?

Yes, in theory this leaves the negotiator free to use whichever style she chooses especially where she is not concerned about the parties' continuing relationship and feels comfortable with this style. However, the facts of this particular problem leave the solicitor for Mr Goodison with little choice, since he is not in a strong bargaining position.

c) who should make the final choice of negotiation style?

Where you are representing a client the original offer or demand in a negotiation, and any concessions, must be approved in advance by him. This suggests that the best approach in this problem is for you to discuss with Mr Goodison what is the lowest figure he is happy to settle, for and by what date. He may be prepared to settle for £4,000 if the money will be made available immediately whereas, if the money will only be made available in two months time, he may not be prepared to settle for so low a figure as he may have to borrow money to tide him over the interim period and will want to cover the cost of such a loan.

As a solicitor you may wish to maintain good relationships with H&G Builders in the hope that the firm will use you again: this may force you into adopting a competitive style since visibly competitive tactics tend to convince clients that their interests are being well represented.

On the other hand, where clients such as Mr Goodison are anxious for an early conclusion to negotiations, perhaps in order to minimise legal fees, or the psychological strain associated with uncertainty, or where there is pressure to reach a settlement before an imminent trial deadline, a non-competitive style is suggested (and usually a co-operative as opposed to a problem-solving one). Pressures result in lower demands, and faster concessions are more easily achieved through the adoption of a co-operative approach.

Possible solutions would include:

- H&G Builders pay for the cost of the electrical work, if it has already been carried out, and/or agree a sum to represent the late completion of the contract
- H&G Builders arrange for the electrical work to be carried out immediately by an agreed electrician, and agree a sum to represent the late completion
- H&G Builders agree a revised final payment
- litigation, with H&G Builders suing on the original contract (on the facts they would probably be successful)
- arbitration

1.10 End of chapter references and additional reading

Axelrod R (1984)	*The Evolution of Co-operation* Basic Books
Berkowitz A (1968)	*Alternative Measures of Authoritarianism, Response Sets and Prediction in a Two Person Game* 74 Journal of Social Psychology 233
Menkel-Meadow C (1964)	*Towards Another View of Legal Negotiation* UCLA Law Review Vol.31 754-842
Osgood C (1962)	*An Alternative to War or Surrender* University of Illinois Press
Raiffa H (1982)	*The Art and Science of Negotiation* Harvard University Press Cambridge, Mass
Williams G R (1983)	*Legal Negotiation and Settlement* West Publishing Co St Paul, Minn
Fisher and Ury (1981)	*Getting to Yes: Negotiating Agreement Without Giving In* Boston, Houghton Mufflin

CHAPTER 2

Conducting a Negotiation - Interpersonal Skills

'In any culture there are established rules about how interaction shall proceed in different situations and between people in different relationships ... (which) cover the kinds of behaviour which are suitable in the situation.'

Sidney, Brown and Argyle
Skills with People (1973)

2.1 The use of non-verbal skills

2.1.1 Listening skills

Negotiation is a process of communication where each side exchanges information with the other in order to achieve a final agreement on specified issues. What is vital to efficient communication however, is that you train yourself to listen extremely carefully to what the other side says. There is often a difference between what you hope, or would like your opponent to say and what he actually says: it is vital to listen carefully to the actual form of words used by the other side. Thus a statement such as 'That is all I have authority to offer' is substantially different from 'I think that is the most I can offer here'; similarly, 'I agree with your proposal' differs substantially from 'That is a very interesting proposal'.

Always remember that there are certain forms of words traditionally used in negotiations which need to be listened to with great care, for their true meaning is not always immediately clear. For instance your opponent may say 'I am not authorised to agree this price'; unless you listen carefully to this statement you may interpret it as meaning that the price referred to is out of the question. An alternative interpretation might be however, that although the speaker is not authorised to negotiate the price, but that someone else is.

The comment 'We are not prepared to discuss that at this stage' may mean that the negotiators might be prepared to discuss it later, and 'These are our standard contract terms' may mean that nevertheless, they are still negotiable. Similarly if your opponent says that his client would find it extremely difficult to meet a deadline it may only mean that whilst difficult, it is, nonetheless, not impossible.

It is believed that although people can speak at the rate of 120 words per minute, they have the ability to process information at a much faster rate (ie at about 600 words per minute). If this is correct the implication is that while your opponent is speaking you can use your spare mental capacity to process the information you receive and make mental (or written) notes about what is said by the other side, and how it is said.

Many lawyers are extremely poor listeners. Research shows that in negotiations, lawyers will often fail to attend actively while their opponent is speaking, thus missing opportunities for vital information gathering about the case being presented by the other side. In many cases this is because they are thinking about how they should respond when next the opportunity arises for them to speak, or because they believe that what is being said is repetitious and a waste of time, or because they are tired, or do not want to hear more about their client's weak position. Where lawyers do not listen carefully they may misinterpret what is being said to them and thus miss opportunities for compromise or settlement.

It is also the case that opposing negotiators do not always express themselves clearly; sometimes their verbal language is contradicted by their body language leading to confusion in the listener. Whatever the reasons for poor comprehension, an effective way of confirming that the message received is the same as the message sent is to restate or paraphrase what you think the other side is saying at the end of each stage of the discussion. So you say:

> 'Well let me just check that I understand what your side is saying. You say that there is evidence that my client wasn't looking where he was going, because he was in a hurry and if the case goes to trial it is likely that damages will be reduced on account of his contributory negligence. For this reason you are suggesting a settlement figure lower than would be normal in such cases. Have I got that right?'

The point here is that if you think the other side is disclaiming liability, while he is actually talking about your client's contributory negligence, you will not be in a strong position to rebut his claim. It may be that having grasped what the other side is saying you will now be able go on to rebut this argument, with evidence that supports your client's case.

As you listen to the other side it may be helpful for you to take notes of what is being said. If you do decide to do this, make sure that you do not become so immersed in note-taking that you fail to attend fully to the other side's argument. It may sometimes be helpful to have an assistant take notes, but be sure to check immediately afterwards that the notes taken accord with your own understanding of what has actually been agreed, and which areas remain to be agreed. Different people will have different interpretations of what has been said, often depending on their knowledge of the preceding facts; if your assistant is unfamiliar with the case, or with the law underlying it, then his notes may be less than useful.

2.1.2 Giving and receiving non-verbal messages

Non-verbal behaviour clearly affects messages sent and received. Abercrombie (1968), an authority on linguistics has said, 'We speak with our vocal organs, but we converse with our whole body'. Thus non-verbal signals play a crucial role in verbal communication. For example, the pitch, the stress and the temporal pattern of your spoken language will convey meaning and give emphasis to certain words as you utter them, indicating for instance whether you are making a serious or a frivolous statement. The same is of course true of your facial and gestural movements, which have the effect of modifying or emphasising your meaning. If you can, take the opportunity to have a video tape made of yourself in informal and formal discussions, and watch out for your own non-verbal mannerisms and signals.

It cannot be emphasised too strongly that non-verbal signals that you are not attending are highly counter-productive in a situation such as negotiation, which depends on agreement between parties. These negative signals include such behaviours as the shifting of gaze away from the speaker, body orientation away from the speaker, yawning, watch checking, sighing and silence. You should make an active effort to avoid them. It is after all perfectly possible to control, at least to some extent, irritating non-verbal behaviours once you have been alerted to their effects.

The importance of maintaining appropriate levels of eye contact with the other person is particularly important. Ideally you should look at his eyes but for no longer than is normal in social conversation (ie probably not for longer than four or five seconds). Do not 'lock' eyes with the other person, as this can be interpreted as a hostile gesture. If you find it difficult to maintain eye contact, focus on the bridge of the other person's nose instead; at a distance of more than four or five feet this will have the same effect. You should never look at people of either gender by focussing on a point anywhere below chin level. If there are several members of the group with whom you are negotiating you should try to make eye contact with every member of the group at regular intervals.

Rapid eye-blinking is normally interpreted by observers to mean that the blinker is experiencing stress. Ordinarily people blink at the rate of four to nine blinks per minute if they are comfortable, and at about eight to ten blinks per minute if they are wearing contact lenses. Thus a blink rate of about twenty per minute will reveal that the person with whom you are negotiating is nervous; this nervousness may be explained by her inexperience or lack of preparation, but equally it may indicate that she is approaching a particularly sensitive part of the negotiation from her client's perspective. If she is using a confrontational style of negotiating this will then be a cue for you to become wary. On the other hand it is possible consciously to control eye blinking, and if you are feeling nervous it may be advisable to monitor your behaviour in order to disguise this.

On the assumption that many people can and do interpret non-verbal signals, try to avoid the temptation to fiddle with your hands, or with any papers or pens on the table as this behaviour is likely to be interpreted by observers as indicating nervousness. So too are such behaviours as ear, eye or nose rubbing, foot tapping or hand clenching. The speaker who holds a hand over his mouth whilst speaking is often thought to be lying or at least uncertain as to his facts.

On the other hand, confidence is expressed by such behaviours as leaning slightly forward when speaking, hands which have the palms turned upwards and visible, nodding gently as the other person is speaking and smiling. An aggressive stance is indicated by exaggerated expressions of amazement or dismay, looking over the tops of spectacles or staring.

2.2 Verbal skills

2.2.1 Questioning skills

This topic is normally discussed in relation to the interviewing of clients (who are often upset or naive), where skilled questioning is essential in order to extract the necessary relevant information. See also Interviewing and Counselling, by Jennifer Chapman, in this series.

However, it is also worth considering questioning skills here. Although in this context your questions will be directed at sophisticated negotiators, you may still be able to use different techniques of questioning to your client's advantage.

Traditionally, questioning styles can be divided into two major categories of 'open' and 'closed' questions. Closed questions are those which require a brief, usually 'yes' or 'no' answer and assume certain facts as being relevant which the negotiator wishes to be clarified. For example, 'Does your client claim that the road conditions were icy at the time?' 'On how many occasions over the past month did your client have access to his children?' A skilled questioner will then use the answer to a closed question to manipulate the other side to confirm a desired position. In the above examples you might respond, 'Oh, I see, then there is no claim that road conditions were poor ' or 'Well, it seems that my client has been quite reasonable in granting access recently', both positions which the other side might not have intended to confirm.

Open questions, on the other hand, are those where the response is less predictable and where the scope of the answer is unlimited. A questioner may be trying to establish rapport or fishing for information. For example, 'What kind of a solution is your client looking for here?' or 'What is the prognosis for your client's condition?' Here you are permitting the other side to introduce new facts, alternative possible solutions, and statements as to liability and compensation which may raise issues which you have planned to discuss at a later stage of the negotiation. On the other hand such questions may give rise to innovative solutions which will cut short the negotiation process and be advantageous to both parties.

As a general principle, well worded, well planned and relevant questions will help to move a negotiation discussion along in a positive way. They will demonstrate that you are listening with attention to the other speaker and that you are motivated to arrive at a mutually satisfactory settlement.

2.2.2 Responding to questioning from the other side

Often, for ethical reasons, certain information cannot be revealed in response to a question from the other side in a negotiation (for example, information which a client has specifically said that she does not want revealed). Other information may need to remain undisclosed at a certain point in a negotiation for tactical purposes (for example, in a discussion over a residence or contact order, your client may not wish to reveal at an early stage that he intends to remarry following divorce). Where these issues arise in the course of a negotiation and you are asked questions which it could be damaging to your client for you to answer, there are various tactics which can be utilised. You can:

- refuse to answer directly, and explain why ('I am afraid that I am not authorised to discuss that issue at present'); and then follow with a question of your own
- say that you will answer the question later in the negotiation ('I will deal with that point later in our discussions, if I may. For the time being I think it would be more helpful if we considered the issue of ...')
- answer only a part of the question, ignoring the remainder
- provide a very general answer ('Yes I do have the witness statements to hand; however I am not sure how helpful we shall find them')
- ask for the question to be clarified ('Can you explain that in a little more detail? I'm not clear what you mean when you refer to the 'undelivered goods'')
- allow the other side to interrupt your answer so that you are never forced to reveal the information which you would prefer not to disclose
- ignore the question and change topic
- depending on your relationship with the other negotiator, you may be able to make a more open, humorous response. For example in response to the question 'What is the minimum amount that your client has authorised you to accept?' you might respond 'Oh come on John, I'm sure you don't really expect me to answer that question at this stage of the negotiation? Nice try though'

2.2.3 Synchronising speech with your opponent in a negotiation

When, as in a negotiation, two or more people are talking they must necessarily take it in turn to speak; normally a fairly smooth synchronisation of speech will occur between two skilled speakers without interruptions or prolonged silences. This is usually achieved by the use of a non-verbal 'code' consisting of head nods, grunts, shifts of gaze and hand movements which permit the speaker to carry on, or indicate that his hearer wishes to interrupt. Thus, at a grammatical pause, a speaker will tend to look up to see if she still has the attention of her listeners. If they are willing for her to carry on speaking they will normally nod their heads, or grunt; if they are not, they may indicate this by interrupting, for example 'If I could just come in on that point, Mary ...'.

If you are speaking, you will normally get helpful feedback about the way your listeners are reacting to to your proposals if you study their faces as you speak; you may find that they indicate such emotions as surprise, disagreement or disbelief at what you are saying. On the other hand, if you are the listener then it is important for you to provide evidence that you are attending to what is being said; you can do this by adopting an appropriate physical proximity to the speaker, and giving the head nods and frequent gaze which are associated with agreement. If you are socially skilled as a communicator then you will be able to deal rapidly and easily with a variety of interaction styles as presented by other negotiators ie you can deal with the over loquacious and dominant as well as those who are nervous and say too little.

It may be that you wish to provide non-verbal reinforcement of the verbal behaviour of the person with whom you are negotiating; research shows that head nods, smiling, leaning forward, looking interested and making encouraging noises are all behaviours that will reinforce a speaker to continue in the same mode (Hinde 1977). Conversely, if you turn away from the speaker, are silent or fail to provide non-verbal signals of encouragement this will have the effect of making the speaker feel awkward and ill at ease and may make him more voluble in an attempt to cause you to interact with him.

2.3 Communication with your client

There are many potential sources of misunderstanding and confusion between client and lawyer and the majority of these seem to arise as a result of poor communication. There is copious research evidence that such misunderstandings have an deleterious effect on the eventual practical outcome of individual negotiations (Williams 1983). Ill informed clients tend to be more unrealistic in their settlement demands and expect too much of their lawyers.

Obviously , clients need to have the legal implications of their cases explained carefully to them and should be informed early on of such issues as the kind of records that they should be keeping and how their actions may affect their claim. They should also be advised on some important non-legal aspects of their case (for example, the financial, emotional, medical and employment implications of the dispute). Clients should of course always be kept regularly informed of the progress of negotiations either by letter, telephone or meeting.

Suggested activities

a) spend five minutes telling a colleague or fellow student something about a recent holiday; they may not ask questions or comment on your account, but must simply listen carefully. Now ask your colleague to spend five minutes retelling the story as accurately as possible. How accurate was this account?

b) now ask your partner to prepare a scenario in which he or she has been injured in a road traffic accident. Elicit the relevant facts by asking a series of closed and open questions for three minutes. Then check with your partner which relevant facts you failed to elicit.

c) for five minutes describe to your partner how you feel about taking examinations, and record this on video tape. Play back the video tape and observe the non-verbal signals that you display. Ask your partner how he interpreted them.

2.4 End of chapter references and additional reading

Hinde R (ed) (1977) *Non-Verbal Communication* Cambridge University Press

Sidney E, Brown M & Argyle M (1979) *Skills With People* Hutchinson

Ury W (1991) *Getting Past No* Business Books Ltd

Abercrombie D (1968) *Paralanguage* Br. J. dis. Comm 3. 55-9

Williams G R (1983) *Legal Negotiation & Settlement* St Paul, West Publishing Co.

CHAPTER 3

Preparation and Planning

'In all negociations of Difficultie, a Man may not looke, to Sowe and Reape at once; But must Prepare Businesse, and so Ripen it by Degrees.'

from 'The Essayes or Councels, Civil and Morall'
by Francis Bacon (1625)

As Bacon pointed out some 350 years ago, before a negotiation actually takes place it is of the utmost importance for a participant to plan all its details in advance. Such issues as location, timing, mode of communication and the extent of the authority of the negotiator must all be clarified and recorded in advance of the event. However, the first priority is the question, is this case a suitable one for settlement by negotiation?

3.1 Recognising which situations are appropriate for settlement by negotiation

One of the major problems for a lawyer is knowing which cases to settle and which cases to take to trial; nationally over 90% of cases are settled without litigation, and using this norm as a guide means that for each practitioner, approximately nine out of any ten of her cases will involve some element of negotiation with another party.

As indicated in Chapter 1, negotiation requires the active involvement of each side to a dispute in order to achieve an outcome acceptable to both parties; it is thus dependent on both parties preferring that their dispute be settled by negotiation rather than by more formal proceedings. However, for tactical reasons solicitors often pretend that they have no interest in settling a case through negotiation, claiming complete confidence in an eventual trial outcome; often the effect of this is for the other side to adopt a similar position.

> 'Bluffing of this sort seriously distorts the real issues, because it precludes rational weighting of the decision whether to settle, and puts an onus on the attorney who opens settlement negotiations.'
>
> (Williams, 1983)

Additionally, lawyers may be tempted to pursue a case to trial for financial reasons. It cannot be stated too strongly that to pursue a case to litigation for the fees it may generate is clearly unethical and improper.

The main advantages to the client of a negotiated settlement are the avoidance of the costs, delay and unpredictability of trial and the availability of a settlement more likely to meet the needs of both sides. This latter issue is of considerable importance when the parties to a dispute hope to continue a business relationship following settlement. Negotiation is not indicated where the plaintiff feels strongly that he wants his 'day in court', where the facts are complex, where there are difficult issues of causation or proof or where the legal position is unclear. Under these circumstances it is generally preferable for a case to go to trial.

3.2 Typical situations appropriate for settlement by negotiation

These include:

- transactions based on voluntary decisions by the parties to do business with each other . These might include, for example, the sale of premises where your client wishes to buy a house at less than the asking price; the discussion of a rent review clause where the landlord is demanding an increase which your client believes to be excessive; the sale of goods to a company where the head buyer is insisting that your client drops the price of his goods, or the company will cease to stock the brand. It may also include large commercial cases where a negotiated settlement is likely to be the first choice for both parties.

- civil disputes, where one party believes that he has enforceable legal rights against another and can, if negotiation is unsuccessful, resort to litigation; here there is at least one involuntary party. Typical examples would include family law issues such as custody and maintenance (negotiation in family law disputes has met with real success and is clearly supported by legal reform proposals), or minor accident or occupiers liability cases where:

    the fact situations are simple

    the defendant is clearly identifiable

    expected damages are modest

    liability is clear

- labour negotiations, which are a hybrid of the first two examples above. They resemble voluntary transactions in so far as they are based on contractual arrangements and involve on-going relationships. However they also resemble civil disputes because there is often a legal obligation to negotiate, and a legal remedy is available in some cases.
- criminal cases, where the practical necessity of negotiation with the Crown Prosecution Service on matters of procedure and evidence frequently arise. In addition there is also often a need to negotiate with your own client, especially as to plea.

3.3 Evaluating your case prior to negotiation

Each set of facts has certain unique factors which will influence the choice of negotiation style, and the success (or failure) of the chosen negotiation procedure. An analysis of these factors is vital to evaluating and preparing your case before the negotiating process can commence. They include:

- the past, present and possible future relationship between the parties. If the parties intend to continue to have an on-going relationship then a co-operative and/or a problem-solving style of negotiation would appear to be the most appropriate. This is often the case with business transactions.

- time availability and limits. If time is short (for example, if the plaintiff is very ill or in urgent need of a financial settlement), a rapid and efficient means of settling a dispute will be required. On the other hand, where a plaintiff is legally aided he may be prepared to wait for a longer period in order to achieve a desired outcome.
- the existence of alternative means to reach the desired solution (not only litigation but also the availability of mediation or conciliation services, for example) may indicate the adoption of a more aggressive negotiation style, for if all else fails the parties may have recourse to these other forms of dispute resolution.
- the needs and interests of all parties. For example, where children are involved in access or custody disputes it is to the benefit of all parties (including the children) to conclude the matter in such a way as to maintain a measure of goodwill on both sides, if this is at all possible.
- the norms of the negotiators. Negotiation styles and strategies differ from one culture to another. For example, it is well known that in some cultures the listed price of an article is a first offer only and any reasonable counter offer by a purchaser will not be refused. In other cultures however, the retail price quoted will be final, and any counter offer will be met with surprise and indignation.

These bargaining norms have evolved over decades, and the same is true of negotiations between lawyers. As between lawyers, regardless of culture, there is an expectation that the parties will act in good faith and that the outcomes of the negotiation process will be based on rational and fair positions. Information will be exchanged on a confidential basis and any factual statements made by either side will be truthful, and not lies.

Equally, however, it is accepted that statements made during a negotiation may be exaggerations of the negotiator's true position, and in some circumstances negotiators may withhold information, or disclose selectively.

Negotiators who do not follow normative codes of behaviour may provoke a hostile response leading to deadlock. If there is a suspicion that the other side is operating according to different norms, then a discussion of these potential differences may prove fruitful.

3.4 Pre-negotiation arrangements and preparation

The type of contact, the location of meetings, the timing of meetings and the content of the agenda for discussion are all issues which may affect the eventual outcome of a negotiation regardless of the individual merits of the cases. Pre-negotiation contacts may occur by letter, telephone or in person.

3.4.1 Contact by letter

Letters are a step towards formality. They have the advantage of documenting positions in advance and can explain a situation economically and with clarity. However they do have some disadvantages, for they provide the other side with time to reflect on a response; they may also involve more of your time, and thus expense, than do telephone contacts.

3.4.2 Contact by telephone

Telephone contacts tend to be shorter than face to face discussions and therefore less stressful. It is always easier to say 'no' in what is essentially an impersonal situation, and the caller always has the advantage of preparation and anticipation. However, the recipient of a telephone call can always reduce this advantage by not making a decision during the conversation, and returning the call after planning a response.

Many lawyers fail to prepare adequately for telephone contacts. Preparation is especially important, of course, if you anticipate conducting all or part of the actual negotiation over the telephone. It is always advisable prior to making (or taking) a call to:

- familiarise yourself with the necessary facts of the case and the applicable law
- prepare a list of topics for discussion as an agenda
- decide what approach will be the most effective for this particular situation
- rehearse the call in advance in your mind
- anticipate the other side's responses and prepare rebuttal comments
- collect any necessary reference material and place near the telephone
- prepare a reason to justify hanging up and calling back if it becomes necessary to rethink the situation

3.4.3 Location

A decision on the location for the negotiation usually comes down to the office of one or other negotiator; there are advantages to both places. If you hold the negotiation in your own office it will save you the time, expense and inconvenience of travel; you will have all your documentation to hand and you can ensure that a proper atmosphere is established, in which the negotiation will take place.

If the negotiation takes place in the office of the opposing side it is easier to leave, and to concentrate on the negotiations without being distracted or interrupted by other matters, since you leave your other work obligations behind you when you leave your own office. You can, moreover, refuse requests for documents on the grounds of non-availability, but you can expect the other side to have all their documents available. One difficulty sometimes encountered if you agree to meet in the office of your opponent is that you may be met by a colleague of the negotiator, who has been 'unavoidably called away'. In such circumstances it is unlikely that the colleague will be as well briefed or indeed have the authority of the original negotiator. If this occurs, it is often better to reschedule the negotiation, since you may inadvertently reveal something of your true position whilst your negotiating opponent will reveal nothing (she has nothing to reveal). You can reach no agreement or concession for she has no authority and can give nothing away.

Other possible locations for meetings that you could consider include a neutral site, or your client's own office.

3.4.4 Who should attend

The question of who should attend a negotiation should also be considered in advance. Sometimes negotiations take place between the barristers for each side alone, sometimes solicitors attend with the barristers and sometimes solicitors will carry out negotiations on their own (for example, in a conveyancing case). Remember, the more professionals who attend, the higher the cost to the parties, and thus the likely financial outcomes must be considered when taking this decision. Remember also that some clients may wish to be present at negotiations and in some cases, for example when negotiating on behalf of a business client, this may be quite appropriate; however, where there is bad feeling between the parties, (as for instance in a divorce case) it will not help matters for the clients to be present.

3.4.5 Your authority

You will need your client's approval before finalising a negotiation on his behalf. Within this overall guideline, however, there are various degrees of authority which a client may delegate to his solicitor, and it is important to identify the precise level of authority during the planning and preparation stage. This authority should preferably be given in writing to protect the solicitor and to prevent future misunderstandings. There are a number of possible alternatives including:

- unlimited authority, where the client wishes her solicitor to have complete control over decision making, subject to her final overall approval

- specific authority, where the client instructs the solicitor specifically in relation to every aspect of the case to be negotiated
- alternative authority, where the client may agree to alternative potential solutions in the event of failure to agree her preferred solution
- no authority, where the solicitor is permitted only to engage in preliminary discussions
- a range of authority may be indicated within which the solicitor may make a final decision, for example in relation to timing

The requirement for authority at an appropriate level actually makes it easier for you to step away from a negotiation, if it seems tactically necessary, on the grounds that you must take further instructions before negotiating further . Finally, make sure that in reaching a settlement the other side is acting with the client's authority or you may find you have problems in implementing the agreed solution (see *Waugh v Clifford & Sons* [1982] 1 All ER 1095).

3.5 Timelines in negotiations

It is often difficult to control exactly when each stage of the negotiation process takes place, but any negotiation plan should include the setting of appropriate times and deadlines. Sometimes your client will put pressure on you to settle quickly, for reasons special to his case; for example, a commercial tenant who has to find alternative accommodation rapidly, a vendor who must complete by a certain date, or a plaintiff who wishes to have his compensation claim settled in time for the family holiday period.

Caution should be exercised before revealing such information to the other side, since this knowledge may strengthen the other party's bargaining position. In this connection, see also Chapter 4 on the Stages of the Negotiation Process.

3.6 Starting your negotiation note-book

Part of your preparation for a negotiation should include developing a note-book in which all the necessary information relating to a specific case is contained. Obviously this will include a summary of the basic facts relevant to the case, as well as details of those issues referred to earlier in this chapter.

For your note book you are advised to use a hard covered ring back binder in which there is a page appropriately headed for each of the following items.

SECTION A

Overview

- list of issues in dispute which are to be negotiated
- clear statement as to client's preferred outcome(s)
- time chart, planning the various stages in the process (this may be subject to amendment as the negotiation process continues)

SECTION B

Facts and figures

documents

- list of available documents
- relevant facts with dates
- evidence such as photographs of injuries, maps, witness statements, police reports, etc
- reports of technical, medical experts etc
- actuarial analyses
- receipts, for example for medical treatment

factual omissions

- any fact deficiencies which need to be made good
- list of questions for interrogatories
- list of documents for which disclosure is sought

notes

- list of meetings to date with notes of time, place and outcomes
- list of telephone conversations to date with list of time and outcomes and copies of notes
- relevant legal rules with authorities

SECTION C

Advance planning

general issues

- characteristics and preferences of other negotiator (if known)
- prioritised agenda for discussion (which may have been submitted to the other side prior to negotiation)
- choice of negotiation style and strategies
- level of your authority to negotiate; initial offer or demand; client's bottom line

detailed preparation

- summary of potentially strong and weak points for both sides
- summary of potential rebuttals
- possible creative solutions
- details of objective criteria against which offers/demands can be evaluated
- planned concessions agreed in advance with client

SECTION D

Notes of negotiation meetings

- notes recording agreement between negotiators
- notes recording details of meetings and telephone conversations with client following initial negotiation(s)
- notes detailing client's final instructions
- notes detailing final negotiated settlement

3.7 End of chapter questions

a) What do you think you might learn from rehearsing a negotiation in advance, and how might you do this?

b) Some litigators are reluctant to introduce the idea of settlement talks for fear of weakening their position, and thereby reducing the possibility of a favourable settlement for their client. What legitimate reasons can you give to the other side for raising with them the possibility of a negotiated settlement , without weakening your position?

3.8 Sample answers

a) What might you learn from rehearsing a negotiation, and how might you do this?

To rehearse a negotiation obviously increases the time involved and therefore the cost of preparation. However if the issues at stake are high or the negotiator inexperienced or apprehensive then it is probably worthwhile.

- the quickest and the cheapest way to rehearse is with the aid of a cassette recorder. Practise making your main negotiation points and your planned rebuttals; you can then play this back to yourself in private and by this means get a feel for the forcefulness of your arguments, the effectiveness of your rebuttals, and your general negotiating manner.

- if the occasion is an important one, ask a trusted colleague or relative to play the opposing role. Here several scenarios can be developed which will reflect alternative ways in which a negotiation can proceed. Again you can tape the mock negotiations and play it back to yourself afterwards to appraise the success of your strategy.
- if a great deal of client money depends on the outcome of the negotiation, or if the negotiation is especially important for some other reason, it might be worthwhile making a video tape of a simulated negotiation, in which you can observe your non-verbal as well as verbal signals.

b) what reasons might you give to the other side for suggesting negotiation discussions?

- this type of matter is normally settled by agreement between the parties (or is best settled this way)
- your firm has a policy of contacting the other side to consider negotiation in these cases
- you represent the defendant who is responsible for what occurred so it is only right that you should make an initial offer
- you have a potentially attractive proposal for their client
- both clients will save money if the matter is settled before trial
- the judge will expect the representatives of both sides to have considered settlement so perhaps you should start now

3.9 End of chapter references and additional reading

Bono De E (1986) *Conflicts: A Better Way to Resolve Them* Penguin

Gold N, Mackie K & Twining W (1989) *Learning Lawyers' Skills* Butterworths

Marsh P (1984) *Contract Negotiation Handbook* Gower Publishing

Sidney E, Brown M, & Argyle M (1979) *Skills with People: A Guide for Managers* Hutchinson

CHAPTER 4

The Stages of the Negotiation Process

'Negotiation is a repetitive process that follows reasonably predictable patterns over time. Yet in legal disputes so much of the attorney's attention and energy are absorbed by the pre-trial procedure and the approach of the trial, that they fail to recognise the important identifiable patterns and dynamics of the negotiation process.'

Williams
Legal Negotiation and Settlement 1983

4.1 Assessing interests

In commencing a negotiation the key question to be answered at the earliest possible stage is 'what are the real interests at stake here?' and to distinguish these from ancillary matters which may not be of real importance to the client. It is of course quite common for negotiators to include fake needs in their negotiation strategy which they will then be prepared to 'jettison' in response to a compromise by the other side.

Negotiators sometimes insist on certain preconditions and make specific demands before a negotiation begins, or before certain concessions can be made. These demands may be about the agenda for the negotiation, or about the date, time or place at which the event will take place. When responding to such demands try to place them in a realistic context; demands as to place and time may be tactically harmless and may be readily conceded if it means that discussions can take place promptly.

You may perceive other demands, however, as being less harmless and you should try to deal with them by ascertaining their underlying purpose. If, for example, your opponent wishes to bring a large negotiation team with her then this may imply a lack of confidence on her part as to her ability to handle the discussion, or may reflect her assessment of her client's case as a weak one. You may find this information helpful in pressing your own client's claim.

Equally of course, she may wish to overpower you with the strength of her negotiating team hoping for a quick agreement; in this case consider your opponent's time constraints and try to use them to your own advantage.

4.2 Preliminaries

At the outset you will need to initiate some kind of effective communication link with the other negotiator, agree the basic facts and exchange the necessary documents. You will also need to obtain agreement on the date, time and place of the negotiation and who will attend it, and you will advise your client of these arrangements. You will clarify with your client the extent of your authority to act on his behalf.

As a result of this process you will have orientated yourself to the basic approach and style of the other lawyer with whom you will be negotiating, and this orientation may be of importance in deciding your negotiation style.

If the meeting is to be held in your office you will need to take the normal steps to ensure that the physical environment in which the negotiation takes place is a helpful one. You will wish to be free of telephone or other interruptions and will operate most efficiently if the room is comfortable (both as to temperature and furniture) and provided with the necessary refreshment (tea and coffee) and other facilities (phone out, paper, photocopying and fax near at hand, and so on). Depending on your negotiating style you will also wish to make your opposite number feel as comfortable as possible (as a co-operative or problem-solving negotiator) or relatively less comfortable (as a competitive negotiator). This latter state can be achieved by manipulation of furniture, blinds and seating arrangements, although the author does not personally recommend this approach.

Imagine that you are now at your first negotiation meeting. The style that you use to conduct this first negotiation meeting will depend on:

- your analysis of your client (see Chapter 1)
- your own personal preferences
- the preliminary or earlier contacts that have occurred between you and the other lawyer

As emphasised earlier (see Chapter 1), it would be misleading to assume that as a negotiator you can adopt a single style throughout the negotiation; in fact, as the discussions proceed you will find that you may need to change style, and hence tactics, to accommodate the changing situation. Research evidence suggests that it is possible for negotiators to switch from one style to another given sufficient encouragement or provocation. Your choice of style should also take into account the impact that your choice may have on the other negotiator. If you chose to be reasonable and co-operative then it may be that the other side will respond with the same style of negotiation; on the other hand if you choose to be aggressive then it is likely that you will be faced with a similar response.

4.3 Basic structure of the negotiation process

It is axiomatic that no two negotiation situations will ever be the same, and therefore there can be no set plan for all negotiations. Indeed the most important aspect of a negotiator's skill is to be flexible and approach each case on its merits. However, in most negotiations you are likely to go through the majority of the following stages, although not necessarily exactly in this order.

4.3.1 Agenda-setting

Unless an agenda has been agreed in advance you will agree with the opposing lawyer the practical issues of how the negotiation will be conducted, what the agenda for the discussions will be, in what order the agenda will be taken and how discussions will be recorded and minuted.

4.3.2 Clarification of the facts

A possible first move is for you, or your opponent, to identify and agree the relevant available facts of the dispute and the law relating to those facts.

This could then be followed by your identification of, and agreement on, any missing or conflicting facts, or differences in documentation. At this point you could seek to resolve such differences through further investigation, and through listening to and questioning the other side.

4.3.3 Setting objectives and opening offers

You may then identify and agree each party's stated objectives; what both sides hope to achieve as a result of the discussions. It is at this point that your choice of negotiating style will first become evident.

- if you are acting as a competitive negotiator you will probably conceal your client's real objectives and/or argue for a maximum settlement for your client, based on the assumption that as an opening position this is only a bargaining point from which you might expect to come down in the final agreement.
- if you are acting as a co-operative negotiator you will be relatively open about your client's objectives, and might open with a proposal which you believe to be fair to both sides. You will probably not expect to move from this suggestion unless it can be shown to your satisfaction that neither party will benefit from it.
- if you are acting as a problem-solving negotiator you will again be open about your client's objectives and probably suggest that there are a number of alternative solutions to the dispute; you will seek, through discussion, to arrange them in an innovative package that will yield maximum benefit to both parties.

Depending on your negotiation style, you will either promote alternative solutions to the problem that will satisfy both parties (co-operative/problem-solving style) or you will put forward as strongly as possible those arguments which support your client's position (competitive style).

4.3.4 Evaluation and repositioning

- you will next assess alternative solutions in relation to the needs of both parties (co-operative/problem-solving style) or you will make strong counter proposals to your opponents position (competitive style)
- you will eliminate unworkable proposals (co-operative/problem-solving style) or use a variety of negotiating tactics to enhance your position and discredit that of your opponent (confrontational style)
- you will generate new proposals (co-operative/problem-solving style) or identify trade-offs and concessions (competitive style)
- you will consider ending the negotiation if the trade-offs are too high for both parties(co-operative/problem-solving style) or if the trade-offs are acceptable to your side although not to the other (competitive style)

4.3.5 Closing

Finally you will need to find a way of closing the negotiation. The alternatives at this stage include:

- adjourning to obtain further information, and instructions from your client
- adjourning to report a final offer from the other side to your client and seek his instructions
- reaching a final agreement as authorised by your client

If the outcome is successful and a settlement has been reached, you will need to check your understanding of the settlement with that of your opponent to make certain that you are in agreement. You must next decide how the settlement is going to be made legally enforceable (if it is), and who will draft the terms of any written settlement.

If no agreement has been reached and yet it appears that there is still some hope of settlement, the best way forward is to agree on an adjournment of the discussion and fix a date and time for a further meeting.

If no agreement is reached and this appears to be a final breakdown of negotiations, you should try to ascertain whether anything can be saved from the discussions as a basis for future negotiation. Try to ensure that you part from the other negotiator on good terms. You will then advise your client accordingly and obtain further instructions in relation to any further attempts at settlement or preparation for litigation.

4.3.6 Follow-ups

- confirm outcomes in writing to the opposing negotiator, your client and all interested parties
- carry out all the relevant practice operations (report writing, filing, billing etc)

4.4 Review

Throughout the whole of the process referred to above, it is helpful from time to time for the lawyers to review the stage that has been reached in the discussions. This is especially recommended if you appear to have reached a deadlock, or there is an uncomfortable silence. A review gives each side the opportunity to compare their original objectives with what has been achieved so far and consider how the negotiation should proceed. This can lead to one or other of the negotiators stating a revised or more innovative position as a potential solution to the problem.

4.5 End of chapter references and additional reading

Foskett D (1985) — *The Law and Practice of Compromise* Sweet & Maxwell

Scott B (1981) — *The Skills of Negotiating* Gower Publishing

CHAPTER 5 Transcript of a Personal Injury Negotiation

The pattern of a negotiation described in Chapter 4 is an essentially linear one, which of course bears some resemblance to reality but does not tell the whole story. In real life it is unlikely that any negotiation will reflect exactly the process outlined in the previous chapter. What would be most helpful to you at this point would be to observe in real life (or on video) a negotiation between two lawyers. However, not all readers will have access to videotaped or live negotiations for observation. It is for that reason that this chapter contains a transcript of a negotiation between two lawyers together with an account of the facts surrounding the case. Some questions are posed for you to consider as you read the transcript, and comments on the style and strategies of the lawyers concerned follow below.

5.1 Facts of the accident

The plaintiff in this case is a young male university student who was knocked down and seriously injured whilst riding home from college on his moped at about 4.00 pm on a June afternoon. The defendant, a lady of about fifty, was driving on a straight road in the opposite direction to the plaintiff when her car crossed over the white line down the centre of the road and hit him head on. The plaintiff was thrown from his moped over the roof of the car on to the pavement on his side of the road and suffered serious multiple fractures, cuts and abrasions and head injuries which have left him with recurrent headaches. There were no other vehicles involved, the road was completely clear and road conditions were good. The defendant was charged with, and convicted of, a road traffic offence (driving without due care and attention) for which she was fined £75 and her license was endorsed.

5.2 Questions for consideration

As you read the transcript through:

- try to identify the negotiation style used at different points
- relate the progression of the negotiation to the linear model in Chapter 4
- decide what mistakes were made by the two negotiators which caused this negotiation to break down
- assess how the participants could have avoided this break down
- identify verbal signals from the plaintiff's lawyer which indicate early on that he is not happy with the way that the negotiation is progressing

5.3 A negotiation transcript

D Thanks very much for coming over today; I hope the traffic wasn't too heavy?

P No, it wasn't too bad. Look, I haven't got a lot of time today, I'm due in court this afternoon, so I do hope that we're going to be able to settle this issue pretty rapidly.

D Well, we've settled a lot of cases like this between us; I don't see why this problem should prove any more difficult than the others.

P Mmmm.

D We've paid £20,000 into court and I think that should cover the extent of the compensation that would be awarded if this case went to trial.

P I'm not altogether sure I can agree with that.

D OK, shall we start by you outlining your special damages?

P Oh, all right; well, actually, they were outlined in the last letter I sent you dated the 25th of the eighth.

D Have they changed since then?

P Not really; as you'll remember they come to about £17,000. The cost of private hospital care in the local Nuffield hospital was £12,500, physiotherapy was about £2,500 and there are some small items to cover like the cost of a cancelled holiday uncovered by insurance and the uninsured excess on my client's vehicle, together with clothes and other items damaged in the accident.

D Why the private treatment?

P Well, it was a very serious injury, and in any case the family had health insurance which is a first claim on any compensation he gets, so I'm assuming here that he is out of pocket for the whole of this amount.

D Is he going to have any more medical bills that you know of?

P Well he may have to go back into hospital early next year to have the pin removed from his upper leg; it seems to be giving him some pain at present and in that case I expect that he would be an in-patient for about a week.

D All seems a bit excessive ... apart from that is he fully recovered now?

P He's been discharged by the hospital and has been having six monthly check ups with the consultant. I think you have Dr Grewal's last letter there which says he had his last check up in June. As you see, it says that he can bend his right leg and move his right arm although there seems to be some deformity of the left scapula, and a twelve inch operation scar down the right thigh. He has been treated by a plastic surgeon for the scar to the upper right cheek and it says in the letter that 'The operation has been successful'. I think that's a bit of an overstatement actually because you can still definitely see something there.

D Well, Dr Skells is a very well known plastic surgeon and I believe that he's pretty reliable; if that's what he says, I'm inclined to accept it.

P Yes, well, the physical disabilities still haven't cleared up either. My client still cannot play squash or badminton and in the cold weather he suffers pain in his right leg at the point of fracture. But much worse than that is the fact that he is still suffering these recurrent migrainous type headaches. They have been troubling him ever since the accident and I think there is no doubt that they were caused by his head injuries. He was unconscious on admission, you know.

There may be other specials for further treatment but I think we've reached a point where the majority of them are out of the way and we can begin to negotiate.

D Is there anything else planned by way of medical treatment apart from the removal of the pin?

P No, not that I know of. I think he's really been very fortunate considering the seriousness of his injuries and the severity of the accident.

D Mmm. I understand he's swimming again.

P Well, I don't know about that; surely you haven't had an observer down at the swimming baths?

D Well, we have had a private investigator take a look at what he's able to do, you know.

P I see. Mmmm ... well I understand that swimming is a very good form of therapy for injuries such as his.

D Yes, I know that, but don't forget he was a keen swimmer before all this happened. It looks to me as though he is getting back into his old sporting interests again.

P It wasn't such a serious interest of his, I think; he was much keener on squash and cross country running.

D Is he claiming any loss of income?

P Oh yes, there is a small sum here. He used to have a part-time job stacking shelves in the University Library at week-ends. The pay wasn't much but there looks to be a total figure of about £400 over the past twelve months for that. I haven't really sat down and worked it out properly yet.

D But surely, Charles, you don't take that very seriously. Here you have a student studying computer science, from quite a well-off family who can afford private medical insurance. He isn't going to spend his career stacking library shelves.

P No, of course not, but this is a loss of income which must be taken into account. It's awfully hot in here John, I think I'll take my coat off. Do you mind if I open a window?

D No, go ahead. Anyway, what do you think the case is worth as a whole?

P Well, taking into account pain, suffering and loss of amenity, together with the specials, I think we're looking at upwards of £50,000 here.

D £50,000! How do you get to that figure from £17,000? That's a huge jump. I can't see any judge awarding anything like that.

P Well, first of all there are the physical problems which make sport difficult for him. Then there's the slight facial scar which is very embarrassing for a young man of that age who is looking to settle down and marry within the next few years.

D His wife would need a magnifying glass to see that scar from what I read.

P The most serious issue is the headaches. This young man is studying computer science; he has to sit in front of a monitor every day, and that's going to be very difficult with these persistent headaches. Just read his affidavit. It says that sometimes the pain is so bad that he has to spend the whole day in bed. He missed one of his examinations this year on that account.

D What subject was that?

P Hang on a minute and I'll check ... oh yes, that's right, it was Maths.

D He didn't do too well in his Maths 'A' levels, did he? Sounds to me like a very convenient headache!

P Well, I don't know about that. Anyway, he's passed the referred examination now. However, if he does less well in his examinations than he would otherwise have done, or even fails them, then his future earnings will be substantially affected. As it is he will entering the job market a year late because if you remember he missed a year's study after the accident. At a time of recession like this, that could prove a very serious disadvantage for him.

D Well, what about his contributory negligence in this case?

P That's a completely new one on me. As I understand it there is no evidence that he was contributorily negligent. Your insured was driving too fast and without care. She failed to look out carefully and collided with my client. The police map shows that he was on the correct side of the road at the time of the collision.

D Yes, but he was pretty near the white line.

P Well, my view is that your insured had had too much to drink at the time of the accident.

D There's no evidence of that.

P How else would you explain an accident like this? The road was perfectly clear, the weather was good, my client was driving slowly as he was just about to enter his own drive. Unfortunately there have been no witnesses found, but obviously the blame rests firmly on your insured. In any case she's been convicted of dangerous driving which puts the burden of proof on her now. There's no doubt there was some lack of care on her part, whatever the cause.

D On the other hand, why wasn't your client watching the road more carefully? He must have seen my insured coming and could have avoided her, if he had been taking proper care of himself.

P Oh come on, John; you know I don't have to show that he took care to avoid all possible bad driving.

D Would it change your position at all if I told you that we had located a witness who says your client was wobbling about all over the road?

P That doesn't worry me. I don't consider that to be crucial. He was on the proper side of the road when he was hit. The police map shows that, so that's all that concerns us.

D And why wasn't he wearing his glasses at the time of the accident? I think I can bring in a expert witness who will testify that without glasses your client would not be able to take necessary avoiding action until too late.

P Look, let's just talk about how this happened. My client was driving on the correct side of the road when he was approached by your insured who swerved over the white line and struck him head on, then continued at speed for a further 750 yards. Now who is really to blame for that situation?

D All right, let's move this along a bit. Let's assume that contributory negligence for not wearing his glasses would only amount to about 10%, what would you estimate the case at now?

P Give me a moment to work it out.

D OK.

P OK, taking into account the contributory negligence at 10% and the severe effect of my client's injuries on his future career opportunities and leisure and social interests, I would total this case up to about £40,000.

D How do you work that out?

P Here we have a young man with a good future before him in computing, and a skilled sportsman who has already lost study time and career opportunities, and may lose more in the future on account of the headaches. He may have permanent brain damage; after all it is still very early to determine the final outcome of this accident ...

D Look Charles I know you don't really believe that your client has serious brain damage; if you did you wouldn't want to settle so soon and you wouldn't be talking about a claim for £40,000.

P Well, I'm only responding to your invitation to discuss matters. Remember this meeting was not at my suggestion. I've dragged all the way here through the rain and I've another meeting on the other side of town in half an hour. I think I've had enough of this discussion.

D Yes, I know that, but you didn't have to come if you thought it inappropriate at this stage. The fact that you're here at this point means you don't really believe that he has serious brain damage. After all, he's back at University now, isn't he?

P Yes, he is.

D And he's getting along OK isn't he?

P Well he failed two exams at the end of his first year there and he stills gets these very bad headaches. His GP has prescribed him some very strong medication for headaches which makes him drowsy and unable to concentrate and may affect his classification when he graduates.

D Yes, but he passed all his second year exams and has done really quite well on his placement; I don't think there's much sign of brain injury.

P Nonetheless, he's still suffering pretty badly and that should be taken into account when arriving at a figure.

D Well, I'd like to find out whether migraines run in his family before I come to any decision on that point; and there's still the question of liability. I think 10% contributory negligence is pretty low here for a young man driving along on a moped without wearing spectacles to correct his vision.

P So how do you assess your liability?

D Well I'd say on the basis of 30% contributory negligence, and the possibility of a causation problem on the headaches the most I could suggest is £25,000, and if you can't discuss that figure I think we'd better call it a day.

P In that case, I think we'd probably better discontinue this discussion. In any case I've got another meeting to go to.

5.4 Commentary on the negotiation transcript

- In this transcript the defendant adopted from the outset a competitive and aggressive style. In the end the plaintiff was forced to give up the discussion in the face of this strategy. However, this could hardly be said to be for the benefit of the defendant, since it is likely that the case may now go to trial.
- There were very early signs from the plaintiff's lawyer that he was not responding well to this strategy, but these were completely ignored. He complained of the heat in the office and the fact that he had another meeting to go to. He was non-committal in response to the early figures suggested by the defendant's lawyer.
- Neither negotiator was entirely honest about his client's case; both were aware of information which was detrimental to their side and neither revealed it voluntarily. The strong point for the plaintiff was the head injuries and their consequences. The strong points for the defence were the fact that the plaintiff may not have been wearing glasses to correct his vision at the time of the accident (although the transcript does not indicate that there is any evidence of this) and that the headaches could possibly have been the consequence of a pre-existing condition.
- The plaintiff's underlying need for financial compensation were never clearly articulated or explained to the defendant's negotiator. There was no attempt by either negotiator to identify innovative options which might have suited both sides.
- Although the negotiation was clearly carried out 'in the shadow of the law' (issues of contributory negligence, causation and res ipsa loquitur are all involved in this case), there was no attempt at an analysis of the legal issues in relation to the facts. Legal points were used as threats, usually by the defence negotiator. For example, the suggestion by the defence that the plaintiff might have had an existing tendency to develop migraine headaches was not developed into a discussion of the thin skull rule.

- Neither side appeared to be fully prepared for the negotiation. This was particularly true of the defence negotiator who had to be reminded of the documents already in his possession which he had not apparently read. It was also true of the plaintiff's representative, who had not prepared any alternative calculations to take into the meeting with him.
- There is some evidence from the transcript that the plaintiff's negotiator felt physically uncomfortable during the negotiation. He was offered no refreshments nor helped off with his coat. The ordinary social niceties were omitted by the defendant's lawyer. This may have been strategic; or it may simply have been an oversight. In either case, the obvious discomfort of the plaintiff's negotiator did not improve the chances of this meeting becoming a co-operative or a problem-solving negotiation.

5.5 End of chapter references and additional reading

Jacker N (1982)	*Effective Negotiation Techniques for Lawyers* National Institute for Trial Advocacy
Williams G (1983)	*Legal Negotiation and Settlement* West Publishing St Pauls, Minn

CHAPTER 6 Case Studies for Negotiation Practice

6.1 How to use this chapter

This chapter includes some negotiation exercises for you to practice the planning and delivery of a negotiation. You can use the earlier chapters in this book to help you decide on a style, plan your strategy and prepare your materials. Start a negotiation notebook (see Chapter 3) to take into each negotiation with you.

You will need to work with a partner as each case study involves role plays for two negotiators. Try to avoid looking at the instructions for your partner, as in real life you would of course be unaware of this information. The role plays are printed on separate pages, and clearly headed, to help you to avoid seeing the other side's instructions.

At the end of the chapter there is an evaluation sheet which you should copy and fill in after participating in each negotiation exercise. This will assist you in evaluating your own performance and that of your partner's in the light of your original planning. For example, did you end up using the negotiation style which you originally intended, or were you pressured into using a different style by the strength of your opponent? Did you achieve the bottom line indicated by your instructions, or did you do better (or worse)? These and other questions are all important indicators of the success or otherwise of your negotiation (remembering of course that in real life there are other circumstantial criteria against which your success or failure may be measured). The evaluation sheet will provide useful feedback not only for you but for your partner, so you should exchange sheets at the end of the exercise and discuss their contents.

Allow at least one hour for each exercise. This will give you 10 minutes preparation time, 30 minutes to conduct the negotiation, and 20 minutes to fill in the evaluation sheet and discuss the outcomes with your partner.

There are four negotiation exercises for you to attempt. These are a vendor/purchaser negotiation for the sale of a house; a husband/wife negotiation over access to children; a negotiation between a garage and a purchaser over the sale of a defective second hand car; and a personal injury case.

Decide which of these exercises you want to attempt and which role you will play before turning the next few pages; this will help you to avoid reading your partner's role by mistake. It would be a good idea to attempt all these negotiations with different partners, if you have the time, to see how you improve. If you can arrange for your negotiation to be videotaped, this will give you even better feedback. Paragraph 6.6 contains the self-evaluation sheet, and you may copy this part of the book as many times as you like.

6.2 The vendor/purchaser negotiation

Vendor

James McCallig has recently given up his post as a lecturer in computer science at a University to develop his freelance activities as a systems analyst.

He and his family presently live in Kent in a modern four bedroomed house with two bathrooms and a fitted kitchen. He now wishes to move to North Hertfordshire where property prices are somewhat lower, and where his wife's family lives. After a long search he has found a picturesque but somewhat dilapidated cottage some distance from the main transport networks, which is on offer at £150,000. If he buys the property at this price it will mean that he can reduce his present mortgage payments by £400 per month during his early years of freelance activity, and purchase a second car for his wife to get around in.

Mr McCallig knows that several couples have expressed active interest in the cottage, and although the vendor has accepted his offer (the asking price), he knows that he will lose the deal if he does not agree to complete by 1 July.

It is important therefore that he sells his present property in Kent with the minimum delay. He wishes to obtain the full asking price (£250,000) for the property and does not intend to sell the carpets and curtains which can be refitted cheaply in the cottage.

James wishes you to negotiate on his behalf with Adam Elliot, a potential purchaser. The date is now 30 April.

This negotiation should take about 30 minutes.

Purchaser

Adam Elliot is employed as a teacher in West Yorkshire. In January this year he was offered a promotion to become the headteacher of a small comprehensive school in Kent. He has accepted the job and put his own house in Yorkshire on the market. He must be in post no later than 1 September.

His present house is a large Victorian stone built property on three floors with six bedrooms, a large garden and panoramic views over the Calder valley. However, the property is not fully modernised and he has been advised that he can only expect to get about £175,000 for this house, although if he were prepared to wait longer he might get more.

Mr Elliot has found a much smaller and more modern house in Kent with four bedrooms and two bathrooms which he does not particularly like, but which suits his immediate needs as he has three teenage children and needs a minimum of four bedrooms. The selling price of £250,000 is in excess of what he can really afford and since there are rumours that there may be a rise in interest rates shortly he would like the vendor to agree to a slightly lower figure. In any event, he would like the attractive carpets, curtains and light fittings to be included in the purchase price, whatever agreement is reached.

Adam has not yet found a purchaser for his own property in Yorkshire, although he is optimistic that he will soon do so, as considerable interest has been shown in it by various potential purchasers. He wishes to move to Kent at the beginning of August.

Adam now wishes you to negotiate on his behalf with James McCallig, the vendor. The date is 30 April.

This negotiation should take about 30 minutes.

6.3 The access negotiation

Wife

Jane has been married to Peter for about 15 years. They have two children, Sarah and Thomas (11 and 9 years respectively). For several years Peter has had increasing outside interests which take him away from home at weekends and on almost every evening of the week. He is involved in local politics, and is a keen rock climber and fell walker. He also helps to run a local youth club and has on several occasions been involved in taking its members abroad on holiday camps. Five weeks ago Jane discovered that Peter has begun an affair with Ellen, who is secretary of the local political party to which Peter belongs. At Jane's insistence, he moved out of the matrimonial home five weeks ago to live with Ellen in a small village four miles away. He has not asked to see the children since leaving.

In August, Peter is going to France on a camping holiday with children from the youth club and he now says that he wishes to take Thomas and Sarah with him. At the same time he has said that regular access arrangements must be worked out soon, as he would like the children to visit him in his new home each weekend.

Jane does not wish the children to go to France as she believes that Ellen will be there and she does not want her children to form a relationship with her. In any case, she thinks Thomas is too young to go as the children from the youth club are all in their teens. Jane is also worried about the general safety of Sarah and Thomas in France and the possibility that they may observe the older children (or their father) in sexual activity. Peter has never been involved in the day-to-day care of his children, and Jane thinks he is not really competent to look after them.

On the regular access point she certainly does not want to be left alone at week-ends without the children. She hopes that Peter will eventually return to the matrimonial home, but fears he will not, and that she might also lose the children.

She asks you to negotiate an arrangement which will satisfy both Peter and herself, keep open the possibility of his eventual return and ensure the safety of her children.

This negotiation should take about 30 minutes.

Husband

Peter has been married to Jane for the past 15 years and they have two children, Sarah and Thomas, aged 11 and 9 years respectively. For some time Peter has been very dissatisfied with his marriage as he has felt that Jane was totally absorbed in caring for the children and had insufficient time for him. As a result, he has become actively involved in local political activities, helps out at a local youth club and has taken up fell and rock walking. Also about two years ago he met Ellen and since then has been involved in an increasingly serious affair with her.

Five weeks ago Jane found out about this relationship and, following a furious altercation, asked Peter to leave the matrimonial home. Peter did this with some relief moving in with Ellen who lives in a small village four miles away. Since moving out Peter has not sought access to the children as he wanted to 'let the dust settle'. He now thinks it is time that he saw them again as he is worried that Jane may turn them against him. He feels that her influence on them is not altogether satisfactory as she seems to be obsessively concerned with their health and personal safety. He feels that he has had a good relationship with his children, particularly Sarah. He and Ellen are going to France on a camping holiday with children from the local youth club in three weeks time and they would like to take Sarah and Thomas with them. Peter wants them to get to know Ellen and hopes that the holiday will provide the beginning of a regular access arrangement.

He asks you to negotiate an arrangement in which the children can come on the camping holiday with him, and on their return, come to stay with him and Ellen each weekend.

The negotiation should take about 30 minutes.

6.4 The dud car negotiation

Purchaser

Robert is a student who has inherited a small sum of money (£3,000) and decides that he would like to buy his first car. In the local paper he sees advertised a Vauxhall Sierra, four years old with a fairly high mileage on the clock. The seller is a small garage called Vince Motors.

Along with some of his fellow students Robert visits the garage and sees the car on the forecourt. The bodywork looks shiny and unscratched and in the road tests the vehicle performed well, showing no signs of any mechanical defects. On his return to the garage Robert asks the owner of the garage, 'Has the car ever been in an accident?' to which the manager replied 'Only just a small bump at the rear which we have put right; nothing to worry about'.

Robert purchases the car and the following week takes it in to a local dealer to have a radio and cassette player fitted. The electrician says to Robert when he comes to collect the car 'This one's been in a bad accident. Looks as though the bodywork's all out of alignment; it needs to be put on the jig'.

Robert also discovers during a bad shower of rain on the same day that the sunshine roof lets through rain as well as sun and that the passenger door has dropped on its hinges.

He returns to the garage, points out the defects and asks for the return of his money. The manager of the garage refuses. 'What do you expect for £3,500, a Rolls Royce?' he says. He offers Robert the opportunity to select another car from the forecourt. Unfortunately all the other cars are more expensive, and in any case Robert does not wish to buy another car from this particular garage. He threatens to report the garage to the local Trading Standards Inspector.

Robert now asks you to negotiate with the garage for the return of his money. At the worst he will accept another car but this time he wants it to be inspected by the AA, at the expense of the garage, before he accepts it. Also he cannot afford to pay any more than the original £3,500, and would like back the £150 he spent on having the radio and cassette player fitted.

This negotiation should take about 30 minutes.

Seller

Vince is the owner of a small firm called Vince Garages. He is a mechanic by trade and the main business of his firm is the repair and maintenance of motor cars. Recently he has expanded by carrying three or four vehicles on his forecourt which are for sale. He usually picks these up at auction, repairs them as necessary and sells them on through advertisements in the local weekly press.

Vince purchases a Vauxhall Sierra for £2,000 which is four years old with a fairly high mileage on the clock, and which has apparently been involved in a shunting accident. He repairs the bodywork and advertises it for sale at £3,500. A group of students come to the garage one Saturday afternoon and have a test drive in the car. One of this group, Robert shows interest in buying it. He asks Vince if it has ever been involved in an accident. Vince replies that it has had 'a bump' but that he has repaired the damage and the car is now O.K. Robert buys the car for the asking price but returns a week later saying that he has been told that the car was involved in a major accident and that he now wants his money back. He also asks for the return of £150 he has spent having a radio cassette fitted in it. Robert also threatens to report him to the Trading Standards Inspector.

In the meantime, Vince has used Robert's money to invest in another couple of second-hand cars which he is currently repairing and hopes to sell for round £4,500 each. One of them is a Vauxhall Sierra of the same year with a lower mileage than the car he sold to Robert.

Vince is worried by Robert's threat to report him to the Trading Standards Inspector. He is also concerned about his claim for a return of his money, as he has not sufficient cash to pay him at present. In addition, although he cannot be confident that the car was not involved in a major smash he has sufficient mechanical knowledge to feel sure that the car is not potentially dangerous, and he is prepared to put right the defects that Robert has identified. Alternatively he will take the car back and exchange it for any of the other models he currently has on the forecourt, providing Robert makes up the cash difference.

Vince asks you to negotiate a settlement of this dispute.

This negotiation should take about 30 minutes.

6.5 The whiplash negotiation

Driver

At 4.00 pm on 20 December Mrs Twining (aged 72) was driving her car home from Sainsways, the local supermarket. The traffic was quite heavy as it was just before Christmas, and she says that was forced to come to a stop in the road outside the supermarket.

As she stopped she was struck from behind by a delivery wagon belonging to Sainsways Stores. She immediately got out of the car to investigate whether there was any damage, but as she did so, became aware of pain in her neck and shoulders.

Mrs Twining was taken by police car to the local hospital where X-rays of the skull, neck and dorsal spine revealed no evidence of bone damage. However, she was fitted with a cervical collar, given pain-killing tablets and told to go home and rest until after Christmas. In January she returned to the hospital to attend a series of six physiotherapy sessions as an out-patient.

By the following March Mrs Twining was still complaining of pain and discomfort and at her solicitor's request was seen by the consultant who reported as follows:

> 'The patient is right handed. The right grip extends at 220-240 and the left at 280. There is hyperaesthesia of the right upper quarter of the body. An electromyogram of the right arm demonstrates grade 1 denervation in the field of the sixth cervical nerve root on the right side. I believe that the patient sustained an injury to the soft tissue of the cervical spine in the accident of 20 December.'

Mrs Twining cannot afford for the case to go to trial and she asks you to negotiate a sum in settlement of her claim against Sainsways Supermarkets Ltd. The average sum currently awarded for such injuries is in the region of £2,500 to £4,900.

This negotiation should take about 30 minutes.

Lawyer

You are an in-house lawyer for Sainsways Supermarkets Ltd. You are handling a claim against the company who, it is alleged, are vicariously liable for the careless driving of an employee who was delivering goods to a supermarket during the immediate pre-Christmas period. The truck driver said in his statement that the traffic was quite heavy but moving at about 15 miles per hour, when the plaintiff, who was immediately in front of him, suddenly slammed on the brakes without any signal or other warning.

The truck driver, who has a clear driving record, is adamant that he is not to blame, and says that 'the old dear didn't know what day it was when she got out of her car. I guess she'd been doing a bit too much wine-tasting in the store'. You have discovered that a firm retailing Australian sherry was in the store at the time, offering small glasses of sherry to potential customers.

Your driver is not willing to accept that he was in any way responsible for the accident as that may affect his employment potential. Sainsways wishes to avoid any adverse publicity. You suspect that the plaintiff's problems are caused by her age rather than the accident, and that the accident itself was not the fault of the Sainsways employee.

You are asked to negotiate a settlement with Mrs Twining's solicitor. The average sum currently awarded for such injuries is in the region of £2,500 to £4,900.

This negotiation should take about 30 minutes.

6.6 Self-evaluation sheet

1 Negotiation Style

What style did you decide to employ when you planned for this negotiation? Please explain why you decided on this style.

....

....

....

....

Were you able to maintain this style throughout the negotiation exercise?

YES/NO

If your answer was NO can you describe what behaviours of your opponent caused you to abandon your preferred style?

....

....

....

....

Did you reveal any information during the negotiation which was valuable to your opponent?

YES/NO

If YES, how did your opponent acquire this information?

....

....

....

....

What style do you think your opponent intended to use during this negotiation?

....

....

....

....

Did you allow your opponent to use his or her chosen style?

YES/NO

If NO how did you prevent your opponent from using her chosen style?

....

....

....

....

Did your opponent reveal any information during the negotiation that was valuable to your client?

YES/NO

If YES, how did you acquire this information?

....

....

....

....

2 Non-verbal signals

Were you aware of giving your opponent any non-verbal signals which s/he might have found helpful?

YES/NO

If YES, what were they?

....

....

....

....

Did your opponent give any non-verbal signals that helped you?

YES/NO

If YES, what were they?

....

....

....

....

3 Preparation

Did you feel that you were well prepared as to both facts and law in this negotiation?

YES/NO

If NO, how would you change your preparation plan in future?

....

....

....

....

Did you prepare a range of alternative solutions in advance?

YES/NO

If YES, what were they?

....

....

....

....

Did you feel that your opponent was well prepared as to facts and law in this negotiation?

YES/NO

If NO, what areas were ill prepared in your opinion?

....

....

....

....

Did you think that your opponent had prepared alternative solutions in advance?

YES/NO

If YES, what were they?

....

....

....

....

4 Outcomes

Did you achieve an outcome that you feel your client would be happy with?

YES/NO

If NO, please explain why not.

....

....

....

....

Do you think your opponent achieved an outcome that his/her client would be happy with?

YES/NO

If NO, please explain why not.

....

....

....

....

5 Future Professional Relationship

Would you be happy to negotiate with this opponent on another occasion, or has this negotiation soured what could be a good professional relationship?

....

....

....

....

Do you think your opponent would be happy to negotiate with you again?

....

....

....

....

CHAPTER 7 Beyond the Basic Approach

7.1 Introduction

In Chapter 4, the discussion of the stages of a negotiation, the point was made that it is not possible for a negotiator to adopt a single style throughout a negotiation. Indeed, as discussions proceed, you may find that you need to change style and hence to change tactics quite suddenly.

Inexperienced lawyers may be at a decided disadvantage in negotiations where their lack of experience makes them vulnerable to some types of negotiating tactics. This disadvantage can be alleviated if you learn to analyse the proceedings to discover which tactics are being used. The purpose of this chapter is to describe some of the special tactics that can be used in negotiations when the occasion demands.

7.2 Making an extreme opening demand

The advantage of the use of this tactic is that an extreme demand makes it plain that, despite your inexperience, you cannot be pushed into accepting a lower settlement than is fair for your client. Moreover, when the opposing lawyer does manage to reduce your figure (as of course he must), he will feel correspondingly better about it than if you had started at a more reasonable figure.

Other advantages of an extreme opening demand are:

- this commences the negotiation at your preferred level; indeed if your opponent has not prepared for the negotiation adequately, he may come to believe that his bottom line is unrealistic and move upwards towards your opening demand
- the chances are enhanced of the end result being higher are enhanced

Beware however that you do not start with so high a demand that it brings the negotiation prematurely to a close. Even if this does not occur, extreme demands can disrupt the negotiation process, and can lead to you having to make large concessions in order to keep the negotiation under way. This in turn will lead to a loss of credibility on your part.

7.3 The ultimatum

The use of an ultimatum is seldom effective as an opening tactic in a negotiation. However, there may come a point in a lengthy negotiation where you feel you need to use this tactic. Perhaps the other side has become increasingly intransigent, and you are increasingly weary; time is going by and you feel that a shock tactic may move the discussion ahead. Of course the risk of issuing an ultimatum is that the negotiation might break down altogether and leave you with no further basis for discussion. Sometimes negotiators faced with the threat of an ultimatum (for example, as a last offer in a lease negotiation or a final settlement figure in a personal injury case) will be prepared to settle, fearing that if they don't accept what appears to be a last offer the case will go to trial and their client may eventually be offered less by a judge.

The effectiveness of an ultimatum may be dependent on:

- the proximity of the figure offered to other similar recent settlements
- the length of time already spent on the negotiation. Thus an ultimatum at the outset of a negotiation (for example, a high opening demand with no room for manoeuvre) is most unlikely to prove acceptable to the other side; however, an ultimatum at the end of a protracted negotiation, (for example a 'take it or leave it', or 'split the difference' proposition) is more likely to be effective. The negotiator for the other side will not wish to abandon all the time and effort already spent in the negotiation, and is more likely to be receptive to a proposal which will finally conclude a matter of which she may have become heartily tired.

However, ultimata do not always succeed in this way. In the negotiation transcript in Chapter 5, the lawyer representing the insurance company says, in response to a suggested settlement of £40,000,

> 'The most I could suggest is £25,000, and if you can't discuss that figure, I think we'd better call it a day'.

This is an ultimatum at the end of an increasingly irritable negotiation. Unfortunately for the insurers, the plaintiff's lawyer in this case responds by saying,

> 'All right, I think we'd better discontinue this discussion ...'

The ultimatum here has produced breakdown., despite the protracted nature of the preceding negotiation.

- the sum or principle at issue

Cases where the sum or principle at issue is not significant and the time available for negotiation is necessarily short are particularly appropriate for the use of an ultimatum. Here the other side may be prepared to accept a final offer for the sake of convenience, knowing that their client will not be greatly disadvantaged by the agreement reached, especially if it is fairly near a reasonable figure.

- the existence of a reasoned argument to support the ultimatum

Where an ultimatum can be supported by a reasoned argument it is more likely to be accepted by the other side, since this allows the opposing lawyer to 'save face'. There is a difference between a 'hard' ultimatum without a suggestion of rationality ('take it or leave it, this is the most you will get') and a 'soft' ultimatum where the negotiator justifies her position by reference to real facts ('I realise how you feel about this, but given the following facts ... I'm sure my client will not go beyond this figure').

- the offering of a concession to support the ultimatum

Similarly where the ultimatum is supported by a concession it is much more likely to be successful. For example, in the transcript in Chapter 5 if the insurer's lawyer had been able to offer immediate payment without further discussion or medical examination, then the plaintiff's representative might have been more inclined to accept. He might have felt, on the specific facts of the case, that it would have been to his client's advantage to conclude matters as rapidly as possible.

Remember that it is always possible to phrase an offer as if it is not an ultimatum, when in fact it is one. Thus you may say 'My client has instructed me to say that he will not move outside the range £20,000 - £25,000'. This then gives the opposition the opportunity to 'choose' the upper limit, which was in fact the figure that the negotiator intended in the first place.

Do not assume that an ultimatum necessarily represents an unchangeable figure; an ultimatum can change upwards. For example, in a case where the plaintiff has a very strong case, his negotiator may say,

> 'My client will accept £5,000 if payment is made before (date); after that date the figure will increase at the rate of 2% per month to cover lost interest.'

Similarly an ultimatum may change downwards, so that in a sale of goods negotiation the plaintiff's lawyer may say,

> 'If the goods are delivered by (date), my client will pay £400 per case; if they are not delivered by that date his offer will decrease by £10 per case per day day for the next ten days at the end of which if the goods are still not delivered, the offer will lapse.'

7.4 The deadlock

Deadlocks can occur at any point in a negotiation and unless carefully handled can signal the end of discussion and the inevitability of litigation, or at the very least further negotiation meetings, as was the case with the negotiation in the transcript in Chapter 5. ('All right, I think we'd better discontinue this discussion; in any case I've got another meeting to go to'). However there are ways out of deadlock, which can be used to your client's advantage:

- try to discuss with the other side why the discussion is deadlocked. For example, in the transcript the defence lawyer might have said,

  'I'm sorry you feel like that; it seems a pity to waste all the good work we've put in today. We've settled other similar matters before, why do you think we can't settle this one?'

- discuss the disadvantages and practical outcomes for both sides, and for the negotiators themselves, if matters remain deadlocked. For example, you might say,

  'Look, if we pack up at this point we'll only have to meet again next month and all this time my client desperately needs some cash to buy a new car and take his family on holiday. He has been through a very trying time, you know - is there no way we can come to some sort of an agreement, at least as to a payment into court?'

- agree to reconsider a particular point if your opponent will do the same. For example, you might say,

  'Look, I think I was being a bit pushy over that demand; let's look at the figures again and see if we can't reach a mid-point agreement; I really don't want to be unreasonable here.'

- suggest that you both take a short break, perhaps for a cup of coffee or a breath of fresh air

- express frustration at the deadlock and seek agreement from the other side on just one issue on which you can both agree (even if it is only an agreement to continue to negotiate), and then try to lead back into the negotiation from that point. While you do this, try to remain pleasant and even tempered.

  'Well, at least we are agreed that the injury was caused by my client; let's have another look at this contributory negligence point and see if we can agree the extent to which your client contributed to his injuries by failing to take good care when he crossed the road. It may be that my client was driving too fast for the road conditions prevailing at the time, but in stepping off the footpath without looking to his left, your client must take some of the blame.'

- empathise with the other side about your joint difficulties in reaching a settlement

  'I know the insurers won't want to go above that figure because of all the other claims in the pipe-line, but this really isn't a 'run of the mill' case, and I think you'll find that they will agree when they realise this.'

- remind the other side of previous successful negotiation meetings you have had
- make a new concession
- arrange a further meeting
- suggest that a third party attend a further meeting

7.5 Walking out

Sometimes negotiators walk out spontaneously, in irritation at the way a negotiation is going. This is ill-advised, as the behaviour will not be a rational or planned decision, but will be an ill-humoured, spur of the moment action. A negotiator who walks out may lose face, and thus bargaining strength. A negotiator who acquires a reputation for regularly walking out will fail to be taken seriously in future negotiations.

On some occasions, however, you can use walking out as a strategy to put pressure on the other side. It is surprising how many negotiators fear that their opponent will walk out as they see this as a sign of their own failure as negotiators; often they will be willing to make quite major concessions to avoid this happening. If you feel that your opponent may react to the threat of walk-out by making concessions, make sure that you give due warning of your planned walk-out so that she can think out the concessions she is willing to make in good time for you to take advantage of them.

> 'If we can't make any more progress than this then I'm really going to have to go, I'm terribly pressed for time.'

7.6 Threats

The success of a threat as a negotiating tactic depends on the extent to which the party being threatened believes the threat. A negotiator may make a threat believable by feigning confidence in carrying out the threat (which may in fact be very difficult to carry out), or by reference to a third party for whose actions the negotiator cannot be held responsible (usually the client).

For example, a negotiator may threaten to take certain actions if her opposing negotiator will not agree to a particular element of his claim. Where this occurs and you are on the receiving end of the threat it is unwise to let the other side get away with threatening behaviour, even if you do not actually believe that she will carry out her threat.

For example, in the transcript in Chapter 5, the lawyer representing the insurers threatens to prove that the plaintiff was riding with uncorrected vision and thus raises the possibility that if the case goes to trial, compensation will be reduced to take account of the plaintiff's contributory negligence.

> 'I think I can bring in a expert witness who will testify that without glasses your client would not be able to take the necessary avoiding action until too late.'

There are various responses that you can make to take the heat out of threats of this nature. They include:

- asking for the threatening statement to be repeated. This gives you (and your opponent) time to think again, and will sometimes demonstrate how ridiculous the threat really is. This strategy may also give your opponent time to rethink and to rephrase her statement in less threatening terms
- remain silent to consider an appropriate response. This indicates to your opponent that you take his threat seriously, and at the same time, may make him feel slightly uncomfortable
- express disbelief or amazement at the statement. This may cause your opponent to rethink her position and tactfully back down

- laugh, as though the threat had been made as some sort of a joke
- act as though you are personally distressed by the statement

In the extract from the transcript above the opposing negotiator might have said in response,

> 'I would have thought, John, that you would know me well enough by now to know that if there were any evidence of that sort I would have revealed it to you at the outset. I am very surprised that you should make that suggestion.'

With luck this response may cause your opponent to apologise or at least change withdraw from the extreme position he has adopted.

- try to make your opponent feel guilty at his own threatening behaviour
- discuss the terms of the threat with the other side to discover whether it is a real one, for example,

> 'Have you any evidence at all to suggest that my client should have been wearing glasses, at the time of the accident?'

- counter the threat with one of your own. This is exactly what the negotiator for the plaintiff does in the transcript, when he says,

> 'Well, my view is that that your insured had had too much to drink at the time of the accident.'

Here the plaintiff's representative responds to the threat of contributory negligence with a threat of his own. However, as you will see from the subsequent discussion between the lawyers, it is at this point that the negotiation goes badly wrong; meeting one threat with another may simply cause ill-feeling and aggression to develop between negotiators. This cannot be to the benefit of either party.

- change the focus of the discussion. This is what the insurers' lawyer does when he responds to his opponent's threatening behaviour by saying,

> 'Let's move this along a bit ... what would you estimate the case at now?'

7.7 The ability to say 'no'

An extremely important technique in any sort of negotiation strategy is the ability to say 'no', and the appropriate manner in which you say it. The first and most basic point to learn is that anything but an immediate 'no' is capable of being translated by the other side as 'yes'.

This rule is easier to demonstrate than to explain. Imagine that you are in the final stages of a negotiation and you propose a figure to the other side. She writes it down, thinks about it for a few moments and then says, 'I don't think I can accept that offer'. The words used formally convey the meaning 'no' but in reality the negotiator's hesitation, and other non-verbal communication communicate the meaning 'yes'.

If an offer is made which you know is out of the question, shake your head as the other side is actually making the offer, and when it is your turn to speak say 'no' as firmly as possible. If you are believed it will save you a lot of time and trouble later on. Try to avoid the mistake which occurred early on in the transcript in Chapter 5 when the lawyer representing the insurers says,

> 'We've paid £20,000 into court and I think that should cover the extent of compensation that would be awarded if this case went to trial',

to which the lawyer for the plaintiff who intends to reject the offer, replies,

> 'Well I'm not altogether sure I can agree with that.'

Perhaps if he had been more definite at this point that he considered that this sum was too low, he could have avoided ending up with a deadlock and walk out after a fruitless and lengthy discussion.

7.8 The use of silence

A really skilled negotiator knows the power of silence. Remember that this is an aggressive negotiating tactic in our culture where people are made uncomfortable by prolonged silence unless they are with others whom they know very well indeed. However, if you understand how powerful silence can be, you can if you wish use it effectively to the advantage of your client (and to the discomfiture of the other side).

Try asking the lawyer representing the other side a question, and, when he has answered it, force yourself to remain silent. He will invariably go on to reveal more about his negotiating position in order to avoid the awkwardness of the silence continuing. His perception will be that your silence is caused by his having failed to answer the question fully, or justified his position satisfactorily. The longer you remain silent the more information you are likely to be able to extract from him.

Similarly, learn to restrain your own tendency to fill in any embarrassing silences caused by your opponent. It is natural to want to respond and to argue your point or your position, but if you can bear to remain silent it will be to your client's advantage. If you cannot simply allow the silence to persist, at least be aware of what is happening and consciously change the topic. You can also force the other negotiator to admit this tactic by saying (preferably in a good humoured way),

> 'I know you hope that by remaining silent you will force me into showing my hand; well, I'm not falling for that one.'

7.9 The lock-in

Another powerful technique for you to to use, and to be aware of, is the lock-in. Here the speaker implies that despite all the risks and the good reasons to the contrary, she is 'locked-into' a position from which she cannot get out. Thus she may say,

> 'I know there is likely to be a risk for our side at trial, but my company is aware of that and is prepared to accept it in order to establish this point.'

or

> 'My client is quite unreasonable. I've told him all the risks he is running, and recommended your offer to him most strongly, but he's just not interested. I suppose he wants his day in court.'

This is a powerful weapon since it implies that whatever the facts of the case, logic of your opponent's argument or the good relationship between the two negotiators, there are powerful external forces which make it impossible to reach a logical settlement. Possible responses to the lock-in are:

- walk out: while this might be an understandable reaction, this is probably inadvisable because the longer you stay with the negotiation the more likely it is that you can persuade your opponent to change her stance, if only slightly
- shift the focus of the discussion, as there may be other issues which need to be considered, and on which you can reach agreement
- challenge the assertion. Do you really believe your opponent's locked-in position? Ask for further details; ask her to explain exactly what her client has said. Attempt to reinterpret her client's instructions in a different light
- empathise with your opponent at having to deal with such a difficult client and suggest that you can mutually reach a settlement that will meet her requirements

7.10 Double dealing

The experienced negotiator may use a variety of gambits to make you feel ill at ease and unsure of yourself in early negotiations. For example, he may:

- deliberately deceive you; for instance, as to the extent of his authority to negotiate, or as to facts and figures. You should always be prepared to verify any statements of fact, either in advance of the negotiation or prior to final settlement

- insult you. He may make patronising or condescending comments such as, 'Are you sure you are experienced enough to handle this negotiation?'
- use delaying tactics (especially common where the negotiator represents an insurance company)

7.11 Questions

a) despite all efforts, some negotiations eventually fail. Is it necessarily a bad thing for a negotiation to fail? What negotiator characteristics maximise the likelihood of failure?

b) is litigation the only possible progression from failed negotiation?

7.12 Sample answers

a) A negotiation may fail for many reasons. Indeed, not all should end in agreement for some cases are inappropriate for settlement by negotiation and need to be tried in court (see also Chapter 1).

In addition, there are a variety of reasons relating to negotiator behaviour which cause individual negotiations to collapse. These include:

- the development of a strongly adversarial relationship between the negotiating parties, where there is a personality clash
- negotiators who argue facts and law instead of exchanging information and discussing issues
- a failure to define issues and focus on the interests of the parties
- negotiators who seek to satisfy their own ego needs, rather than the needs of their clients
- negotiators who become emotionally involved in the process, leading to irrational and hostile behaviour

- negotiators who simply exchange extreme opening demands
- negotiators who are only able to focus on the position of their own client and who ignore the position of the other party and the other party's negotiator

b) Litigation is no longer the only option available where negotiation has failed. There is a growing interest in this country in alternative dispute resolution processes, including:

- mediation

Mediation is private, voluntary and if agreement is reached can be enforceable as a contract. A mediator is a neutral party acting as a go-between, assisting communication and negotiating between parties in conflict. The term mediation is often confused or used interchangeably with ...

- conciliation

This is most often used in commercial and family disputes, and has been practised in this country for some years. In family matters there will usually be a matrimonial lawyer and a probation officer who will mediate between the parties who are present. Where agreement is reached it will often require court approval (for example, a consent order).

Legal aid is not available for mediation and conciliation, and thus this process is available only to a limited number of people.

- arbitration

Arbitration is similar to litigation although the proceedings are less formal and held in private. The arbitrator is appointed by the parties and may sit with specialist assessors. The process is basically adversarial and decisions are binding on the parties. Arbitration tends to be used in commercial cases where its use has either been agreed in advance (by clauses in contracts or the terms of a collective agreement), or once conflict has developed between the parties.

CHAPTER 8

Improvement and Self Evaluation

'In discussing interpersonal relations ... avoid losing contact with the level of common-sense thinking ... common sense contains much psychological theory'.

Heider 1958
'The Psychology of Interpersonal Relations'

8.1 Introduction

By this point you will have had the opportunity to learn something about the negotiation process, to 'observe' a negotiation in action, and, together with a partner, to practice negotiating using some case studies.

The purpose of this chapter is to give you some suggestions on how you might improve on the interpersonal skills which inevitably underpin your negotiating style. Remember, the entire range of behaviours involved in negotiation is based on what is essentially a small set of behavioural skills, that is, primary or first order interpersonal skills, such as listening, speaking and understanding non-verbal communication.

8.2 Self-assessment

By the time you have reached this point in the book you will have gained sufficient experience to realise how important communication skills are in a legal transaction such as negotiating. Different people have different levels of interpersonal skills and it is important to be able to assess yourself as a basis for further self-improvement.

You could draw up a master list of communication skills that you feel are important in negotiating in order to help you assess your own levels of competence, or if you prefer you can use the one below. Whichever method you employ, remember that it is important for you to be really honest about yourself in answering; remember also that nothing is gained by being too self-critical. Try to spread your scores across the scale as much as possible, rather than huddling in the middle for safety. The purpose of such a checklist - either your own or the one below - is to give you the opportunity to learn from your past mistakes and to improve on your performance.

8.2.1 Self-assessment checklist

After each statement, use the following rating scale to indicate how you assess your own level of ability:

1 quite poor; needs considerable improvement

2 only moderate; needs improvement

3 quite good but still scope for some improvement

4 competent; only fine tuning required

5 excellent

Listening skills

I can:

listen without impatience

listen actively

interpret tone and speed of delivery

use silence effectively

remain calm in the face of threats or ultimata

identify 'lock-in' tactics

'listen' to non-verbal forms of behaviour

Oral skills

I can consciously:

use different tones of voice and speeds of speech to convey my intentions

speak clearly and concisely

open up a deadlock situation by questioning

say 'no' effectively when I need to

deal appropriately with threats and ultimata

create a climate which helps my opponent to listen actively

give information which is:

- accurate
- complete
- appropriate
- well organised
- supported by relevant examples

summarise and reach effective conclusions

treat the listener with courtesy

be responsive as to whether the listener comprehends

Body language skills

I can:

make appropriate eye-contact with others

control my body movements to convey an intended message

make appropriate gestures to convey an intended message

read the body language of the opposing negotiator

When you have gone through this checklist, you should be able to identify which of the three main areas of interpersonal skills (listening, oral and body language) require further improvement. You can then use the suggestions in the text below to help you improve.

8.3 Improving your listening skills

8.3.1 Listening to words

Obviously the ability to interpret and draw conclusions from your opposing negotiator's behaviour includes having the ability to listen actively to the actual form of words that he or she uses during the negotiation. If you feel that your listening skills require improvement, try asking yourself the following questions:

- is my listening posture sufficiently relaxed yet alert? How alert do I look? (This affects how alert you feel.)

When negotiating, sit up (or stand) straight, don't slump in your chair or avoid eye contact with your opposing negotiator. Look eager and interested.

- am I so concerned with 'saying my piece' when the person to whom I am 'listening' is speaking, that I am unable to concentrate on what she is actually saying?

If so, this will give you the appearance of being inattentive, and worse still, it may make your response quite inappropriate when at last you do speak.

- am I bored and do I lose concentration during a lengthy speech by my opponent?

If this happens to you, it may give the impression that you are day-dreaming. Avoid this by trying to make regular contributions to the discussion, if only to summarise what has been said up to that point.

- do I find myself intuitively trying to modify what the other negotiator has said, in an attempt to make it consistent with earlier positions that he has adopted?

If you find yourself doing this, beware, for your opponent may just be inconsistent.

Always remind yourself, however, that if you are looking for cues to your opponent's intentions from what he says his verbal behaviour is easily controlled and despite all your efforts you may be deliberately misled by misrepresentative statements.

8.3.2 Listening' to your opponent's non-verbal behaviour

Non-verbal behaviour, on the other hand, is usually more difficult to control, and your opponent's emotions and attitudes can 'leak out' through her non-verbal behaviour, if you know how to interpret it. As a negotiator you will need to look beyond the surface content of what is being said to consider the motives, attitudes and intentions of your opposing negotiator. This process of interpretation is so necessary to human existence that in adults is is developed to a point where it occurs sub-consciously. This activity is referred to by psychologists as 'person perception'; this simply means having the ability to 'listen' to other people's physical behaviour as a clue to their real intentions.

In order to be able to respond appropriately and effectively to the other side in a negotiation you must be able to perceive their intentions accurately. Research (Davitz 1964) has shown that people who are sensitive to emotional expression in others have two other abilities: they are better able to discriminate (and thus interpret) pitch, loudness and speed of voice in another speaker, and they are better able to express their own emotions in a way which leads others to interpret them accurately.

The commonest sources of error in interpreting other peoples' behaviour are:

- stereotyping, that is, ignoring differences between individuals and regarding any member of a class or grouping as identical (for example, 'all Scots are mean with money')
- assuming similarity, that is, attributing to others characteristics which you yourself possess (for instance, ambitious people will

often believe that everyone else is equally ambitious, and will thus be motivated to act competitively towards them)

- assuming intentionality. There is a temptation to think that others' actions are deliberate, but to think that one's own actions arise from accident or error (for example, *you* intended to deceive, but *I* was mistaken in what I said)
- the locked-in effect. We assume that our initial impression of others is correct and we often ignore any further information, even if it is to the contrary, in order to maintain consistency of approach. If your past experience of a particular negotiator is that he generally fails to prepare in advance, do not always assume that this will be the case in the future. He may suffer a change of heart and catch you unawares

An effective way to improve your skills of person perception is for you personally to become more self-aware, that is, more aware of the way that you stereotype and make assumptions about others. Another is to take careful note of the behavioural cues which indicate the intentions of others. Facial expressions are the most important aspect of body language because the face is mobile, flexible, and is highly visible. Visual expressions are capable of conveying quite accurate information about personal feelings. Additional information about a person's attitudes and beliefs may be derived from her general appearance (for example, clothes, accessories, hairstyle and make-up), which has been deliberately chosen to convey a message about that individual. When you try this exercise remember to bear in mind the earlier 'caveats' about stereotyping and making assumptions.

You can also improve your person perception skills by forcing yourself to to keep an open mind and receive further information before you reach a decision about the other side's motives and intentions. When you are on the train or out shopping think consciously about the judgements you are making about other people on the basis of minimal cues and try to test them out objectively. Concentrate on increasing your awareness of cues and increase your ability to listen actively, not just to the words that are spoken but also to how they are spoken.

Once negotiation begins, a new set of cues become available. Voice tone is a reliable indicator of how your opponent feels about what he is saying, especially when combined with speed of speech and volume. Anger and excitement often cause speakers to talk faster, louder and at a higher pitch while passive emotions result in slower than normal speech, with low volume and pitch.

Remember that people tend to look up as they reach the end of what they want to say; this is a useful indicator because skill in timing speech to avoid interruptions and awkward silences is important for a negotiator.

Actively attempt to engage in eye contact in order to show interest and attention and a positive friendly approach to the other speaker Conversely, eye contact is normally lower if one negotiator dislikes the other, or the negotiation has reached a stage which the speaker finds difficult or embarrassing. If you visibly nod and smile while listening, at the same time keeping your gaze under control, this should be effective in building rapport and establishing a good working relationship with your opponent.

8.3.3 Improving listening skills

You can improve your listening skills to help you to interpret the behaviour of others, by training yourself to:

- look actively for cues in your opponent's behaviour
- identify what those behavioural cues actually mean
- decide on the cause(s) of the behaviour
- consciously avoid being influenced by first impressions
- consciously avoid evaluating your opponent, or his client, on the basis of social class stereotypes
- regularly practise your assessment of behavioural cues, as an aid to person perception

8.4 Improving your oral skills

8.4.1 Oral messages and 'hidden messages'

It is important to realise that by your own oral behaviour you can actually set up active barriers to listening in your opponent. If she receives from you the 'hidden message' that you are attempting to manipulate her, or that you believe yourself to be superior, or that your mind is made up on a particular issue, then the effect will be for your opponent to switch off and concentrate on defending her own position. There is research evidence (Argyle et al 1970) which demonstrates that people are especially sensitive to hidden messages which convey information about what the speaker thinks about himself, his listener and about the relationship between himself and his opponent.

If you want to improve the hidden messages that you convey in the course of a negotiation, try to avoid behaviours such as name dropping, or standing or sitting obliquely so that your gaze is averted from your opponent, avoid being overly judgmental in response to what your opponent has to say, and talking too much about your own needs. In the negotiation transcript in Chapter 5, when Robert's negotiator makes the suggestion that he has suffered brain damage as a result of the accident caused by the defendant, the defendant's negotiator replies,

> 'Look Charles, I know you don't really believe that your client has serious brain damage; if you did you wouldn't want to settle so soon and you wouldn't be talking about a claim for £40,000.'

Here, John attacks the plaintiff's negotiator by making a judgmental statement about the issue he has just raised. In effect, he is 'rubbishing' the position adopted by Charles whose response is to terminate the negotiation very shortly after. The hidden message of this behaviour is that John feels superior to, and critical of, Charles, and as a result Charles responds defensively, bringing the negotiation to an end.

If you want the opposing negotiator to like you, try some of the following tactics:

- as far as possible, be open and personable. For instance you might admit that you are feeling anxious about the negotiation (if indeed you are)
- show liking for your opponent, if you can. This is the most powerful way of ensuring that you are liked in return and works with most people, especially the insecure
- emphasise some similarities between yourself and your opponent, for example, through similarity of speech

8.4.2 Persuasive styles

There is plenty of psychological evidence to support the notion that good interpersonal skills help in persuading another to adopt a particular point of view. Various persuasive styles exist. One typology defines three approaches: the facilitative style; the dominant initiating style; and the logical style. In this typology:

- the negotiator who chooses a facilitative style encourages, compromises, shows concern, and expresses friendliness and warmth in order to achieve change. However, she may also be gullible, over-optimistic and too easily satisfied
- the negotiator who acts as an dominant initiator presses vigorously for results. She tries to influence others by giving orders, issuing challenges and by being generally threatening. She may also create the impression of being dogmatic and overbearing, and if taken too far this style can be counter-productive
- the negotiator who adopts a logical style, as the name implies, appeals to logic as a basis for her line of argument; she presents facts, quotes authorities and refers to rules and regulations as the foundation for her proposals for change. A possible weakness of this style is that its user may have so much faith in her own logic that she fails to see that others are unable to understand or appreciate it. She can, therefore, be overly rigid or 'nit-picking' on occasion

These categories are by no means mutually exclusive and one style is not considered to be superior to another, for each has its own strengths and weaknesses. Perhaps the best approach is one that combines elements of all three styles, the balance between each depending on the circumstances.

You should be aiming to present yourself to the opposing side as a likeable and helpful person, whose objective is to reach a fair level of agreement within a reasonable time. Establish rapport with your opponent through good humour, mastery of the details of the negotiation and common sense.

8.4.3 Dealing with anger

Active emotions such as anger and anxiety tend to make people speak faster, louder and at a higher pitch. If your opponent makes you feel angry, try to control your response by speaking slowly, and by concentrating on keeping the tone of your voice relatively low. If you respond like this you will encourage your opponent to be more reasonable, and you will be left with credit points for not having responded angrily.

If your opponent becomes angry during the course of the negotiation do not make matters worse by trying to interrupt or shout him down; instead, try to listen to what he says, taking care to give the impression that you are paying attention to his point of view, while at the same time ensuring that you keep a tight control over your non-verbal behaviour. While you are listening, try to work out why the speaker has become so angry. Make sure, however, that your silence does not become so noticeable that it might be interpreted as provocative.

8.4.4 Positive verbal signals

A positive approach to a negotiation, which emphasises the pleasant rather than the unpleasant aspects of the situation, is most likely to be effective. Tell the other side what you can agree (rather than what you cannot) Use as few negative words as you can get away with and try to use concrete terms rather than vague generalisations.

Try to create a climate in which your opponent will feel happy to listen to what you have to say. This can be achieved by avoiding boring speeches with long sentences; instead try to break up what you have to say into short sections, and give your opponent the opportunity to participate in a dialogue, rather than simply listen to a monologue. Make sure that your communication is genuinely a 'two-way street'.

People who are amusing can often maintain a listener's attention and interest much more effectively than those who are not. However beware, not all of us are naturally amusing and it is only too easy to lose your credibility and be regarded as a bore if your attempts at humour fail to make your opponent laugh with you.

8.5 Improving your body language skills

8.5.1

Gestures and postures together make up body language and reveal a great deal of what may have been left unsaid. While facial movements may show what someone is thinking, body movements will show how strongly it is felt. Anxiety and stress are particularly easily read from shifts of posture and frequency of movement.

Gestures are defined as movements which are confined to one or two parts of the body (the arm and the hand for instance). Gestures are learned body language, easily copied and just as avoidable.

On the other hand, a posture is a position assumed by the whole body: it is controllable, but it is also very easily affected by what psychologists describe as behavioural contagion (that is, copying the body language of another without being aware that you are doing so). Where a negotiation is going well the postures of the negotiators will often be complimentary to each other, in 'mirror image' positions. Where one negotiator leans expansively back in his chair, the other is likely to imitate the movement, often subconsciously, if the negotiation is going well. Mirror imaging rarely happens where negotiators are feeling antagonistic or hostile towards each other. If you consciously adopt a mirror imaging strategy, this is likely to give your opponent a 'comfortable' feeling that you are essentially in agreement with him.

Combined postural and gestural changes are less easily imitated or copied. They are very revealing about what an individual is feeling, and how strongly he feels it. Thus, anxiety and stress are often indicated by shifts of posture and restless or repetitive bodily movements (these include hand or foot tapping, fiddling with jewellery or clothing, face rubbing, restless walking about and so on). If you lean forward when sitting or perch on the edge of your chair you will be understood by most people as eager to please and enthusiastic. If you hold your back rigid and sit unusually still, you will convey to most people an attitude of rigid self-control and authoritarianism. If your physical posture is relaxed this will be interpreted by observers as meaning you have a relaxed personality.

Posture can also communicate something about the power balance between negotiators. For example, leaning forward towards your opponent can mean that you have a positive attitude towards him. However, be careful, because if you are perceived as leaning into your opponent's 'personal space' this can be interpreted as domineering and authoritarian.

8.6 Conclusion

A great deal of this chapter is no more than everyday common sense, applied to the transactional context of two lawyers negotiating. However, do not make the mistake of disregarding it. Many lawyers who fail to be reflective and self-analytic about their interpersonal behaviour find themselves in difficulties in their dealings with professional colleagues and with their clients. Having read this book, it is hoped that you are now better able to recognise and evaluate your own interpersonal behaviours and thus better able to control these, to the benefit of your clients and yourself.

8.7 End of chapter references and additional reading

Argyle et al (1970)	*'The communication of superior and inferior attitudes by verbal and non-verbal signals'* Brit J Clin Psych Vol 9, 222-231
Bishop S & Taylor D (1991)	*50 Activities for Interpersonal Skills Training* Gower
Burnard P (1992)	*Communicate!* Arnold
Dainow S & Bailey C (1988)	*Developing Skills with People* Wiley
Davitz J P (1964)	*The Communication of Emotional Meaning* New York McGraw Hill
Pattison P (1986)	*Developing Communication Skills* Cambridge University Press
Peel M (1990)	*Improving Your Communication Skills* Kogan Page
Rixon S (1986)	*Developing Listening Skills* Macmillan

CHAPTER 9

Comments on Case Studies

9.1 How to use this chapter

In Chapter 6 you were presented with some case studies to use as a basis for negotiation practice with a partner, with a self-evaluation sheet, for you to assess how well you achieved your objectives in each negotiation.

This chapter contains a short comment on each of the case studies for you to compare with your own negotiation note book, strategies and outcomes. You will learn most from this chapter if you attempt the case studies first.

9.2 The vendor/purchaser negotiation

9.2.1 Background

This case study outlines a common situation appropriate for negotiation, where there is a voluntary decision by the parties to do business with each other. In this case there is little likelihood of the parties doing business with each other again, but there is a possibility that each will continue to use the same negotiator to represent them in subsequent sale and purchase situations if they feel satisfied with the way matters have been handled on their behalf. Time is relatively short in this instance as matters must effectively be concluded within 10 weeks. There is no alternative means of reaching the desired outcome other than by the negotiation process.

In practice it is possible that this type of negotiation may be conducted, at least in part, by the contracting parties themselves. For the purposes of this case study it is assumed that matters will be dealt with entirely by the negotiators acting on their clients' instructions. This particular case study has already been used by several cohorts of students and trainees, who have achieved a surprising variety of outcomes for their 'clients'.

Pre-negotiation contacts are likely to have occurred by letter or 'phone and for the purposes of this exercise it is assumed that the negotiation meeting will take place in the office of one or other lawyer.

9.2.2 Your negotiation note-book

A possible skeleton for a negotiation note-book appears in Chapter 3 at paragraph 3.6. At minimum, your note-book for this negotiation should have included:

- a list of issues for negotiation

In this case study, there are four possible issues for consideration. These are:

a) the purchase price

b) the agreed date for the exchange of contracts

c) which furnishings are in question (eg carpets, curtains, light fittings, etc)

d) the estimated value of furnishings

While the price of the vendor's property is the most substantial issue for negotiation, it is clear that the other issues are not free-standing. If the date on which contracts will be exchanged cannot be agreed, then the sale will fall through because there are competing purchasers for the cottage in Hertfordshire (remember that the vendor must sell rapidly if he is to complete on the cottage by 1 July). On the other hand, the potential purchaser has not yet sold his property in Yorkshire and this may make him a more risky buyer.

- details of the client's preferred outcomes

Each negotiator will have obtained instructions from his or her client as to the main issues and cannot exceed those instructions. In any event, whatever the final outcome of the negotiation it will still need to be ratified by the clients in the form of the contract for sale. In this case, the purchaser's preferred outcome is to purchase for less than the asking price, keep all furnishings in the house and exchange contracts sometime in mid-July. On the other hand, the vendor's objectives are to sell for the asking price of £250,000, exchanging contracts no later than the end of June and taking all his furnishing with him.

- a time chart

The issues need to be settled fairly rapidly if the conveyancing procedures are to be completed by 1 July. This meeting between the negotiators will be the first but ideally it will be the only meeting. If it appears that the purchaser cannot meet the vendor's demands then the vendor will need to find an alternative purchaser very rapidly and the purchaser will have to seek an alternative property. Perhaps in each case an alternative (another purchaser or property) is already being actively pursued.

- documents and notes

The major documents required here are details of the property for sale; the furnishings in question (perhaps with an estimate of their second hand value); and notes of the client's instructions with the dates on which they were agreed.

- prioritised agenda for discussion

The first point to be resolved by the negotiators is the order in which the issues should be discussed. Most students commence by discussing the price of the property, but really it is the date on which contracts can be exchanged which is of greatest importance to the parties. Both parties are committed to the purchase of some property, somewhere, within a prespecified time and financial range.

- summary of potentially strong and weak points for both sides

Vendor

Strong points

The house he is selling meets the requirements of the potential purchaser as to size and locality and is in broadly the right price range.

The house he intends to purchase is chain free.

Weak points

He is short of money and thus needs to get the asking price for the house. He wants to remove the furnishings for refitting in the cottage.

He is in a hurry to complete on his purchase by 1 July.

There are rumours of a possible rise in interest rates.

Purchaser

Strong points

He is not in as great a hurry as the vendor, and can hold out until September if necessary.

He does not particularly like the vendor's house and what is more, there are plenty more on the market if this falls through.

Weak points

He has not yet sold his own house and may need to get a bridging loan to complete this purchase (especially if he completes by the end of June).

He cannot really afford the asking price.

He needs the carpets and curtains as he will be short of money following his move from the North to the South.

- possible creative solutions

The vendor might be persuaded to take only some of the carpets and curtains as the cottage is much smaller than the house he is leaving. In this scenario, either the vendor or the purchaser could agree to make the choice as to what stays and what leaves with the vendor.

The vendor might be persuaded to sell the furnishings to the vendor; this would save him the cost of having them altered and refitted and would save the purchaser the full costs of refurnishing.

- objective criteria against which any agreement can be evaluated

These could include lists of sale prices of other similar houses in the area; evidence of the second-hand value of those items of furnishing to be discussed.

- planned concessions agreed in advance with the client

Vendor

Possible concessions by the vendor might include (in order of priority):

a) he leaves some of furnishings if the purchaser agrees to complete by the end of June

b) he leaves all of furnishings if the purchaser agrees to complete by the end of June

c) he sells some or all of the furnishings if the purchaser agrees to complete by the end of June

d) he reduces the asking price by £5,000 if the purchaser agrees to complete by the end of June and sells some or all of the furnishings

e) he reduces the asking price by £5,000 and he leaves some of the furnishings (to be agreed) if the purchaser agrees to complete by the end of June

f) he reduces the asking price by £5,000 if purchaser agrees to complete by the end of June, and he leaves all the furnishings.

Purchaser

Possible concessions might include (in order of priority):

a) he agrees to pay £240,000 for the property, exchange contracts in mid-July and keeps all the furnishings
b) he agrees to let some of the furnishings go if contracts are exchanged in mid-July at an agreed sale price of £240,000
c) he agrees to let all furnishings go if contracts are exchanged in mid-July at an agreed sale price of £240,000
d) he agrees to exchange contracts at the end of June for a purchase price of £238,000 but retains some furnishings
e) he agrees to exchange contracts at the end of June for a purchase price of £238,000.

9.2.3 The negotiation

- your preferred negotiating style

Your preferred negotiating style will reflect your appraisal of the situation and your own personality. Viewed pragmatically, given that you may have to negotiate with the same lawyer on another occasion, a co-operative or problem-solving approach seems sensible in this situation.

- agenda setting

The five issues for negotiation referred to in paragraph 9.2.2 above need to be agreed and, if possible, prioritised (that is, agree the order in which they should be discussed).

- setting objectives and opening offers

Agree the parties' mutual objectives (see paragraph 9.2.2 above). If you are acting co-operatively, or as a problem-solver, you will be frank about your client's real objectives in relation to time, money and furnishings. If you are negotiating competitively you may not reveal all of them at this stage and may open with an extreme demand. For the vendor an extreme demand might be £250,000 and completion by 30 June and for the purchaser, an offer of £230,000 and completion in mid-July.

- evaluation and repositioning

Promote alternative solutions as listed above (paragraph 9.2.2), or hold firm on your demand. If you adopt the latter approach it is likely that the purchaser will be forced to withdraw and seek property elsewhere as his negotiator is not instructed to settle at this level.

- closing

Most students negotiating this problem adopt a co-operative or problem-solving approach and settle on a date for exchange of 30 June, a figure of between £240,000 and £250,000, and split the furnishings between the parties on an agreed basis. Some negotiations do end in deadlock and walk-out. These are usually where the negotiators have adopted a confrontational approach.

9.3 The access negotiation

9.3.1 Background

This is a much more complex negotiation than the vendor/purchaser negotiation, including as it does issues which impinge on the interests of at least five different people (the wife, the husband, two children, and a third party). Whilst the husband might be able to enforce his rights of access through the courts, it is probably in the best interests of all parties if matters are settled in private between them.

In this case study, unlike the first one, the parties are going to have to continue to have some form of on-going relationship for some time to come, certainly until the children are old enough to make decisions for themselves. For this reason, both the negotiators would be likely to hope to establish at least some element of goodwill between the parties. Note however, that unlike the vendor/purchaser negotiation, here one of the parties (the wife) is an involuntary participant in the negotiation.

There is no particular pressure or time here. Although Peter would like a quick decision regarding the holiday arrangements, this is not essential, and in any case need not pre-determine the general access arrangements which can be negotiated later on.

Pre-negotiation contacts are likely to have occurred by letter or phone and for the purposes of this exercise it is assumed that the negotiation meeting will take place in the office of one or other lawyer. Because this is a highly charged emotional issues it would probably not be appropriate for either of the parties to be present at the negotiation.

9.3.2 Your negotiation note-book

At minimum, your negotiation note-book for this negotiation should have included:

- a list of issues to be negotiated

These will include:

a) whether either of the children can go on holiday to France with Peter and Ellen

b) if they can, what arrangements should be made for accommodation and general care during the holiday

c) the frequency and duration of access visits in the future

d) accommodation and general care arrangements for the access visits

- details of the clients' preferred outcomes

Jane would prefer that the children do not go abroad with their father, and that regular access visits do not last a whole week-end, and/or do not occur weekly.

Peter's preferred outcomes would be that he can take the children away to France and see them regularly, each week-end, on his return from holiday.

- a time chart

Whatever access arrangement is agreed should be acceptable to the parties on a mid to long-term basis. However, since the children have not seen their father for about three months it is probably desirable for their sake that some interim access arrangements are made for the immediate future. The question of the holiday trip (just three weeks away) also needs to be resolved more quickly although this could be dealt with separately from future access arrangements.

- documents and notes

The major documents required here are statements from each client of relevant events with dates; details of the children's ages; client's instructions and level of authority; any notes of earlier meetings.

- summary of potentially strong and weak points for each side

Wife

Strong points

The age of the children.

The fact that the proposed holiday is outside the UK.

The fact that Peter and Ellen have only recently begun to live together (it might be suggested that the relationship is not yet stable enough to be 'formalised' in relation to the children).

Weak points

Peter has a legal right to access to his children (unless and until this right is removed by a court).

Husband

Strong points

He has a legal right to access to his children.

The length of relationship with Ellen (two years).

In practice Jane may be pleased to have some help with the children on a regular basis.

Weak points

He may be on weak moral ground, since he left his family to cohabit with another woman with whom he was already having an adulterous relationship.

He wants to take the children out of the UK.

Having the children every week-end might be described as excessive in terms of 'reasonable' access.

Ellen may not be as anxious as Peter is to have the children for the whole of each week-end.

- possible creative solutions

A range of possible solutions will consist of variations in the frequency and length of regular access visits, possibly combined with an agreement about the holiday in France, although these two issues are capable of separate negotiation. For example,

Both children can go on holiday with Peter and Ellen

Only one child can go on holiday with Peter and Ellen

Neither child can go on holiday with Peter and Ellen

Both children can go on holiday with Peter and Ellen, but only one day each week regular access is agreed

Both children can go on holiday with Peter and Ellen, but only fortnightly access for the weekend is agreed

Neither child can go on holiday with Peter and Ellen, and only one day each week, or one weekend in two, is agreed as regular access

- details of objective criteria against any offers/demands can be evaluated

These could include the relevant legal rules governing the right of a father to access to the children of his marriage and their corresponding right to have access to him; details of recent court decisions on similar contested access cases.

- planned concessions agreed in advance with the client

These might centre on a trade-off between regular access rights and allowing the children to holiday with Peter and Ellen (see above under 'possible creative solutions').

9.3.3 The negotiation

- your preferred negotiating style

Bearing in mind the interests of the parties this case clearly calls for a co-operative or problem solving style; the use of a competitive style of negotiation would not be in the best interests of the children.

Your client's interests should be clarified at the outset of the negotiation. Here the main concern is to reach an agreement incorporating access arrangements which are acceptable to Peter and Jane, and in the best interests of their children. In the absence of any evidence to the contrary, it is assumed that it is in the children's interests to maintain a regular contact with their father. The question of the holiday in France with Peter and Ellen is really an ancillary issue.

During the negotiation itself, the negotiator representing Jane may not wish to be too specific about her particular anxieties in relation to the children's welfare, but might perhaps focus her arguments on the children's young ages, the recent upset in their lives and the need to maintain stability in a known environment.

The negotiator representing Peter will need to emphasise the reliability of his client, the need for his children to maintain a regular relationship with him and the safety of the proposed expedition to France.

Whichever side you represented as a negotiator in this case you should have assessed the many possible solutions referred to above, eliminated the unworkable ones and come up with a reasonable solution which is fair to your client, and in the children's best interests. You should then have adjourned the meeting to report your proposals to your client, and hopefully, to receive her or his agreement.

If both clients agree to the negotiated settlement, then you would have to agree with your opposing negotiator who would draft the terms of any formal agreement between the parties. If no agreement had been reached then you would need to agree a date for further discussions and obtain new instructions.

9.4 The dud car negotiation

9.4.1 Background

A number of Sale of Goods Act issues are raised by this problem. It may be that Robert has a cause of action in contract against Vince. Nonetheless, neither client has either the desire or the funds to go to trial, as the sum of money at issue is not a large one; this is an eminently suitable fact situation for a negotiated settlement. It is extremely unlikely that either party will wish to do business with the other again. It is also unlikely that Robert will wish to be represented again in this type of situation, although Vince may find himself needing representation again, especially if he increases his trade in second-hand cars.

For these reasons the negotiators here could choose to use a competitive style of negotiating without necessarily adversely affecting the interests of their clients. In this regard this negotiation is quite different to the two previous case studies.

9.4.2 Your negotiation note-book

You should have listed the issues in dispute here with a clear statement of your client's preferred outcomes.

- the issues to be determined here include:

  the actual physical condition of the vehicle

  whether the physical condition of the vehicle was misrepresented to the purchaser

  whether the physical condition was so misrepresented as to give rise to a breach of contract

  whether Robert is entitled to some form of recompense

  if he is, what form should that recompense take (free repair; cash equivalent; replacement vehicle)

- the client's preferred outcomes

In this problem no doubt Robert's preferred outcome would be to get his money back, which presumably would have to include the cost of the fitting of the radio. He has also been involved in other expenditure (for example, taxing the vehicle for a period in which he did not drive the car, since it was returned before a full tax month had elapsed) and these issues could be used as the basis for making demands or offering concessions.

Vince's primary aim would be for Robert to exchange the original car for another (possibly more expensive) vehicle.

- a time chart

While there is no urgent time pressure here (Vince has the money and Robert has some form of transport), no doubt both parties would like the matter cleared up with relative speed. A meeting arranged for the near future would obviously suit both parties.

- documents and notes

The major documents and notes required here are:

Robert's receipt for the vehicle and subsequent work carried out

any evidence of defects in the vehicle (expert's report/ photographs)

estimate of necessary repair costs

verification of the dates of the various transactions

notes on client's instructions

notes on relevant legal rules with authorities

9.4.3 The negotiation

- your preferred negotiating style

You may have decided to adopt a competitive negotiation style for this case study; if so, you would have been wise, having agreed your agenda for discussion with the other side, to open with a high initial demand on the assumption that if the other side takes the same attitude (which may happen simply because you initiated this strategy) you are likely to reach a mid-point which would probably be acceptable to both parties.

The first issue for discussion is clearly the physical and mechanical condition of the Vauxhall Sierra purchased by Robert. From the facts given in the case study, there is no independent expert's report to be relied upon in relation to the condition of the vehicle. However, it could probably be confirmed easily enough whether, as alleged, the sun-roof lets in rain and the passenger door needs to be rehung.

In the light of the age and cost of the vehicle it is unlikely that these faults alone would give rise to a finding that the vehicle was not of merchantable quality. (At this point a break in the negotiation might occur, until such time as an expert's report on the condition of the vehicle can be obtained.)

Robert's lawyer should have argued on his behalf that he needed a car urgently, that the Vauxhall was unsafe and that Vince should replace it immediately with one of the cars on his forecourt regardless of the difference in price and together with compensation for the cost of fitting the radio. A combination of threats (Trading Standards, action for breach of contract) and ultimata might have accompanied this approach, if a competitive stance was being adopted.

Vince's lawyer would probably respond by arguing that the car, while suffering from some minor defects, was not basically unsound. Vince would offer to put the defects right himself at no cost to Robert. He would have argued that there were no grounds for breach of contract or the involvement of Trading Standards as the vehicle was in a reasonable condition in view of its age and price; he would also have argued that Robert had the opportunity to test drive the vehicle and should have noticed any defects at that point. Vince's lawyer should stress that as far as his client was aware he had spoken the truth when he said that the vehicle had been involved in a 'bump'; there was no intention to misrepresent the seriousness of the accident and no evidence that the accident had in fact been any worse than that.

Through a variety of concessions and trade-offs the two negotiators should arrive at a point which would be satisfactory to both clients. Various different outcomes have been arrived at by students negotiating this problem in the past. The following are some examples of the solutions they finally achieved through negotiation. These outcomes are listed in what would probably have been a descending order of satisfaction to both the parties involved:

- Robert purchases a second car from Vince at a higher price, making up the difference in value between the two. Vince pays the cost of an AA inspection of the second vehicle, prior to purchase, and compensates Robert for the cost of installing the radio in the original vehicle. The legal costs are shared equally between the parties.
- Robert purchases a second car from Vince at a higher price, splitting the difference in value between the two vehicles with Vince. The legal costs are borne by Vince.
- Vince repairs the original vehicle at no cost and compensates Robert for his time and trouble with a sum of £50. The legal costs are borne by Vince.
- Robert returns the original car to Vince who repays the £3,500 in three monthly instalments. Robert waits, then buys another car from another dealer. The legal costs are split equally between the parties.

9.5 The whiplash negotiation

9.5.1 Background

This is a dispute concerning a relatively minor accident. The defendants (Sainsways Stores) wish to avoid any publicity, as does their driver. The plaintiff cannot afford the case to go to trial and wishes to have it settled out of court. The fact situation appears to be relatively simple, the defendant is clearly identifiable and the damages are likely to be modest. All these characteristics point to a case eminently suitable for settlement by negotiation.

It is unlikely that the parties will have any further relationship of value, and the plaintiff's lawyer will probably not be asked to represent her again (with the possible exception of making her will). The lawyer representing Sainsways, may wish to make a good impression on his client since it will be to his advantage to be retained by the company on future occasions. These circumstances are not suggestive of any one particular negotiation style, and it would depend on the preferences of the negotiators which style each adopts.

Time may be a factor for the plaintiff here. Mrs Twining is not a young woman and it may be to her advantage for the matter to be settled soon.

9.5.2 Your negotiation note-book

- the issues in dispute

  The cause of the accident (whether due to careless driving by either party, for example lack of signals from plaintiff or lack of due care by defendant's driver).

  The cause of the injury complained of (for example, old age, or whiplash injury, or both).

- the client's preferred outcomes

  For the plaintiff, a reasonable figure (say £3,500) in compensation, agreed quickly.

  For the defendant. a low figure (say £1,500) in full and final settlement with no admission of liability and no publicity.

- documents and notes

  The major documents required here are:

  statements from drivers
  medical report(s) on plaintiff
  witness statements (if any)
  police report (if any)
  vehicle report(s) (if any)

- summary of potentially strong and weak points for either side

Plaintiff

Strong points

The defendant's liability can be implied from the fact that he ran into her vehicle from the rear.

The medical expert's report shows injuries consistent with whiplash damage.

Weak points

The plaintiff cannot afford for the case to go to trial, so it must be settled.

The plaintiff is old and infirm, and would make a poor witness.

Because she is old and infirm there may be an implication that she is a poor driver.

The defendant would probably make a good witness.

Defendant

Strong points

He has a clean driving record.

He has suggested that the plaintiff may have been intoxicated.

The possibility that the plaintiff's injury was not caused by the accident but is attributable to her advanced years.

The possibility that the plaintiff might be considered too elderly to drive safely.

Weak points

The defendant ran into the plaintiff from the rear.

There is no evidence to support his claims of the plaintiff's intoxication.

9.5.3 The negotiation

Observations of students and trainees negotiating this problem indicate that usually the negotiator representing the plaintiff uses a co-operative or problem-solving style, while the negotiator representing the defendant tends to use a more competitive style. Perhaps this is because it appears, at least on the face of it, that the defendant is in the wrong, and thus more assertive tactics are required to make his case.

Where there is a conflict between a competitive and a co-operative lawyer, the competitive lawyer often achieves the best deal for his client, providing that he can persuade his opponent to continue the negotiation and not to walk out on it. In this particular problem, the plaintiff has nowhere to go if her lawyer walks out of the negotiation and, as a result, usually comes off badly in the final settlement.

The defendant's lawyer can raise a variety of issues which may strengthen his case, for example, the possibility that the plaintiff was intoxicated, or that the injuries which it is alleged she has received are in fact simply a symptom of old age and caused by arthritis. The defendant can point to his clean driving record, the fact that the traffic was moving very slowly at the time of the accident and the fact that the plaintiff is an elderly lady whose driving skills may well have become impaired by age.

The main task for the plaintiff's lawyer is to emphasise the basic facts as proved: that the plaintiff was run into from behind, an accident for which a defendant is normally held to be responsible, and that as a result he caused the whiplash injury for which the plaintiff seeks a reasonable sum in compensation. An appeal to criteria of fairness may be effective together with a reminder that the driver and the employer are both insured. The plaintiff's negotiator might also point out that any adverse publicity would be bad for Sainsways, a company that prides itself on its service to the public, and it would be better to settle the case immediately for a sum which is fair to the plaintiff and in line with current awards for similar injuries.

There is little scope in this case for innovative solutions to the dispute since the only issue to be agreed is that of a sum in compensation. However, an agreed figure of less than £2,000 for the plaintiff would indicate some weakness on the part of her lawyer in the face of the defendant's allegations.